D1284989

Scott Foresman

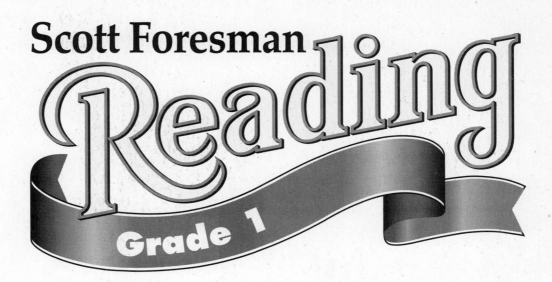

Reading

Grade 1

Leveled Reader Resource Guide

Independent Reader Resource Guide for 1.1–1.6

Scott Foresman

Editorial Offices: Glenview, Illinois • Parsippany, New Jersey • New York, New York
Sales Offices: Parsippany, New Jersey • Duluth, Georgia • Glenview, Illinois
Coppell, Texas • Ontario, California

ISBN: 0-673-59667-2

Copyright © Addison-Wesley Educational Publishers, Inc.
All Rights Reserved. Printed in the United States of America.
This publication, or parts thereof, may be used with appropriate
equipment to reproduce copies for classroom use only.

10 11 12 13 V039 10 09 08 07 06 05 04 03

Table of Contents

Independent Reader Resource Guide Page 209

Unit 4 Favorite Things Old and New (cont.)

Unit 5 Take Me There

Unit 6 Surprise Me!

Introduction

The goal of *Scott Foresman Reading* is to help children not only become better readers in today's classroom, but also to build a love of reading that lasts a lifetime. Children who are having difficulty reading at grade level or reading fluently often develop negative attitudes about reading and themselves. Providing children with reading materials they can and want to read is the first step toward developing fluent readers. The Leveled Readers are a series of high interest, accessible materials that were developed to help children experience the joy of successful and meaningful reading. The Leveled Reader Resource Guide contains easy-to-use instructional plans, graphic organizers, Leveled Reader practice pages, the Scott Foresman Leveling System, and assessment forms that will help you select Leveled Readers appropriate for children's abilities; instruct and support children before, during, and after reading; and assess their performance level.

About the Leveled Readers

There are 360 Leveled Readers in the *Scott Foresman Reading* program that are written one to one and a half grades below grade level. Set A is Easy. Set B is Easy/Average. For each Student Edition selection, there is a corresponding Set A Leveled Reader and a Set B Leveled Reader. Each one focuses on the same target comprehension skill, tested selection vocabulary, and theme as the corresponding Student Edition selection. The Leveled Readers increase in difficulty within a grade and from grade to grade. As children's reading abilities develop, they can begin reading texts with longer and more complex sentences, more pages, fewer illustrations, and more challenging concepts.

Grade	Number of Pages Per Leveled Reader
Grades 1–2	8–16 pages
Grades 3–4	16 pages
Grades 5–6	16–24 pages

See the Scott Foresman Leveling System on pages 205–206 for more information about how the Readers are leveled and to help you select Readers that match children's reading abilities. (There are also Set C/Challenge Leveled Readers, which provide literature and activities for children reading at or above grade level. Each Set C Leveled Reader is linked thematically to a unit in the Student Edition and gives children additional opportunities to expand target comprehension, vocabulary, and critical thinking skills. Instructional plans for Set C Leveled Readers can be found in a separate Leveled Reader Resource Guide.)

Great care and attention were given to create Leveled Readers that are age appropriate and appealing to children for each grade level. The Leveled Readers provide children with a good mix of fiction and nonfiction texts in a variety of genres, such as fantasy, folk tale, realistic story, historical fiction, narrative nonfiction, biography, and how-to books. Many of the Leveled Readers for Grades 1–3 use predictable patterns of rhyme, rhythm, and sentence repetition to facilitate reading fluency. They include art on every page to ensure a good match between picture and text and to maximize comprehension. In all grades, there is a lively blend of humor, surprise, and novelty—characteristics that are very attractive to readers in Grades 1–6.

About the Independent Reader Resource Guide

Beginning on page 210, you will find teacher resource materials and teaching suggestions for the Independent Readers.

Using Leveled Readers

The Leveled Readers can be used to meet the diverse needs of your classroom in a variety of ways:

- as a means of developing fluency and reading skills and strategies for all children,

- as a substitute for the corresponding Student Edition selection for children who are reading below grade level,

- as a reinforcement of the corresponding Student Edition themes, tested selection vocabulary, and target comprehension skills for children reading at or below grade level,

- as a choice in Guided Reading groups,

- as a choice for self-selected reading,

- as a choice for shared reading,

- as a choice for a read aloud,

- as a choice for choral reading or to be performed as Readers Theater,

- as a choice for take-home reading,

- as a choice to be used in conjunction with the Instructional Routine Cards,

- and as a text for assessment of oral reading and other reading skills and strategies.

Using Leveled Reader Practice Pages

Beginning on page 141, you will find Leveled Reader practice pages. There is one practice page for each Leveled Reader. These pages contain comprehension questions set in a test format that will help you assess children's understanding of the Leveled Reader and the target comprehension skill. At least two questions on each page are linked to the target comprehension skill. These pages will also provide test-taking practice.

Use the Leveled Reader practice pages after children have read the Leveled Reader in conjunction with the after reading activities suggested in the instructional plans.

Guided Reading

The instructional plans in the Leveled Reader Resource Guide were developed to be compatible with a guided-reading approach. This approach can be used with small groups of children who are reading at a similar reading level. Use the following routine to guide children before, during, and after reading.

- Select and introduce an appropriate Leveled Reader to the group.

- Have each child read (softly or silently), while you listen, assess, and provide support as needed.

- After reading, reinforce reading skills and strategies, assess comprehension, and help develop fluency by having children reread the text.

The goal in the guided-reading approach is to have children read independently, silently, and, above all, read for meaning.

Managing the Classroom

When you are using the Leveled Readers with individual children or in small groups, you will need to keep the other children engaged in independent and meaningful learning tasks. Establish different work stations around the classroom where children can be working on different tasks simultaneously. Display a work board that indicates the work stations and tells which children should be at each work station. Explain what task or tasks are to be done at each station and give an estimate of how long children should work there. Alert children when they should rotate to new stations and change their station assignments on the work board. Develop a classroom routine regarding the work stations and the rotation among these work stations so children can read and work more independently.

Work stations you can create are:
- Listening Work Station
- Phonics Work Station
- Technology Work Station
- Writing and Language Work Station
- Independent Reading Work Station
- Cross-Curricular Work Station

Using the Leveled Reader Resource Guide

Each Leveled Reader has its own instructional plan in the Leveled Reader Resource Guide, but all plans follow similar before, during, and after reading routines.

At a Glance

1 Links to the Student Edition Each Leveled Reader is linked to a Student Edition selection and focuses on the same target comprehension skill, tested selection vocabulary (the group of tested words is divided between the A and B Leveled Readers), and unit theme. See the Table of Contents to match up the Leveled Readers with their corresponding Student Edition selections.

Before Reading

2 Motivating the Reader Create interest in the Leveled Reader by building background and connecting to what children already know. Suggestions are given for using pictures, videotapes, classroom discussion, graphic organizers, writing, art activities, or simple science experiments to prepare children to read.

3 Preview and Predict Preview the Leveled Reader by walking children through the book. Encourage children to make predictions about what happens in the story or what information they will find in the book. Then suggest a purpose for reading or have them set their own. Point out selection vocabulary and any unfamiliar words or expressions that might be important to understanding the book.

During Reading

4 Guiding Comprehension Have children read the Leveled Reader, either softly or silently, to a specific point in the book or the entire book. Then use the questions provided as needed to support and assess children's comprehension.

5 Ongoing Assessment Listen and watch for children to use effective reading strategies as they read. See the Instructional Routine Cards that discuss the reading strategies that good readers employ. Use the If/Then statements provided to help children develop better reading strategies and build self-awareness and confidence about the good reading strategies they do use. Make notes about children's reading performance, using either the Observation Checklist/Progress Report on page 207 or Taking a Running Record on page 208.

6 Model Your Thinking If children have difficulty with the target comprehension skill, then use the Think Aloud model provided to help children understand what the skill is, why it is a useful skill, and how this skill can be used to understand the Leveled Reader better.

After Reading

7 Revisiting the Text Children will better comprehend the text and develop fluency by rereading the Leveled Reader independently, with a partner, or in a small group. Activity suggestions are given to help children organize their thinking, respond to what they've read, and demonstrate their understanding. See also the Leveled Reader practice pages beginning on page 141.

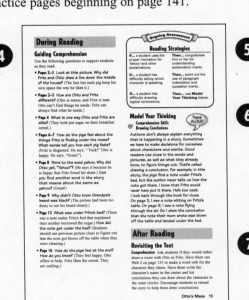

Using the Graphic Organizers

Graphic Organizers can be found on pages 130–140. This set of eleven graphic organizers can be copied onto plastic transparency sheets and used on an overhead projector or copied onto paper for children to use as worksheets. Suggestions are given in the instructional plans for ways to customize and use these graphic organizers.

Assessing Performance

If/Then statements are provided in each instructional plan to help you assess and assist children as they read the Leveled Reader. The Leveled Reader practice pages provide comprehension questions set in a test format. Use the assessment forms on pages 207 and 208 to make notes about children's reading skills, strategies, and behaviors as they read.

- **Observation Checklist/Progress Report** (p. 207) Allows you to note the regularity with which children demonstrate their understanding and use of reading skills and strategies. You can use this assessment form several times throughout the year and compare the results to track a child's progress.

- **Taking a Running Record** (p. 208) Tells how to take a running record so you can calculate a child's reading accuracy and reading rate. (See also the running record sample on the next page.)

Use these assessment forms along with the Scott Foresman Leveling System on pages 205–206 to help you decide whether a child can make the transition to reading materials at the next, more challenging level (child consistently reads at an independent level with an accuracy rate of 98% or better), needs further practice and guided instruction with materials at the same level (child reads at an instructional level with an accuracy rate between 91–97%), or needs targeted instruction and intervention with materials developed for a lower level (child reads at a frustrational level with an accuracy rate below 90%). See the Assessment Handbook for further ideas and forms to help you assess children.

Taking a Running Record

The sample on the next page shows the miscues a child made while reading aloud. See page 208 for more information on taking a running record and assessing the results. Use the notations in the sample to identify the kinds of miscues the child makes while reading. Count the number of errors and subtract them from the total number of words to find the number of words the child read correctly. Divide the number of words correctly read by the total number of words to find the child's accuracy rate. If the child makes the same error more than once, such as mispronouncing *exactly* twice, count it as one error. If possible, tape-record the child reading so you can check your running record. Calculate the reading rate by dividing the total number of words by the number of seconds the child took to read the text. Multiply by sixty to find how many words per minute the child can read. End by having the child retell or summarize the text, so you can assess his or her comprehension of it.

Running Record Sample

Fritz and Otto drew a line down the middle of their (cozy) house. Fritz lived

side

on the right. Otto lived on the left. Fritz kept his things neat. Otto's things were

very

not ~~exactly~~ neat.

/klen/

Fritz kept his things clean. Otto's things were not exactly clean. Fritz could always find what he needed. Otto could never find what he needed.

But Fritz and Otto did one thing the same. They both made their breakfast

H

cereal sweet with sugar. (sc) That was how their mom always fixed it. So Fritz and Otto shared the sugar jar.

—From *Otto's Mess,*
Leveled Reader 62A,
Grade 3

Total Number of Words: __93__

Number of Errors: __5__

Accuracy Percentage Score: __95%__

Reading Time: __70 sec__

Reading Rate: __80 wpm__

Miscues

Omission The child omits words or word parts.

Insertion The child inserts words or parts of words that are not in the text.

Substitution The child substitutes words or parts of words for the words in the text.

Mispronunciation/Misreading The child pronounces or reads a word incorrectly.

Hesitation The child hesitates over a word and the teacher provides the word. Wait several seconds before telling the child what the word is.

Self-correction The child reads a word incorrectly but then corrects the error. Do not count self-corrections as actual errors. However, noting self-corrections will help you identify words the child finds difficult.

$$\frac{93-5}{93} = \frac{88}{93} = .946 = 95\%$$

$$\frac{93}{70} \times 60 = 79.7 = 80 \text{ words per minute}$$

1A Come Back!

by Judy Nayer
Leveled Reader 1A
Genre: Animal Fantasy
Level: Easy

Summary

A big, shaggy dog looks all around a deserted farm for his animal friends. As he walks around the barnyard, he wonders where all the animals have gone. He soon finds out that the animals are giving him a surprise birthday party!

Leveled Reader Practice

After children have read *Come Back!,* use Leveled Reader practice page 141 to assess their understanding of the Leveled Reader and the target comprehension skill. Additional after reading activities are provided on page 11.

At a Glance

Links to the Student Edition

☞ **Comprehension Skill:** Context Clues

Selection Vocabulary: *away, come, will*

Program Theme: The World Around Us
Unit Theme: Take a Closer Look

The dog looks everywhere for his animal friends. When he takes a closer look, he sees they are giving him a surprise birthday party.

Before Reading

Motivating the Reader
Build Background About Go Away and Come Back

Ask children what they do when they want to play with someone. Invite volunteers to tell what they do and what they say. Then suggest a conversation children might have on the telephone or at the door with a friend's older relative. "Did Cara go away? Will Cara come back?" Invite children to repeat the sentences, using their friends' names. Ask children to explain what *away* and *back* mean.

Preview and Predict

Have children scan the cover, text, and illustrations. Encourage them to use picture clues and familiar words to predict what the story is about. Prepare students for reading by asking:

> Who do you think is the main character in this story? How do you know? What do you think the dog wants to know? As you read, notice what the dog asks and what the dog is thinking.

Point out selection vocabulary, using gestures to indicate the meaning of *away* and *back*.

During Reading

Guiding Comprehension

Use the following questions to support children as they read.

- **Page 2** **Who is the dog looking for? How do you know?** (He is looking for the hens. The bag of grain has a picture of a hen on it. Also, the dog imagines the hens running away and asks where they are.)

- **Page 3** **What does the dog say about the ducks? Let's point and say the words.** (Read aloud with children as they point and read, remaining silent as they read *away* and *come back*.)

- **Page 4** **What does the dog think happened to the goats? How do you know?** (He thinks the goats climbed over the fence and ran away. You can tell by looking at the part of the picture that is in a thought bubble.)

- **Page 5** **Who is the dog looking for?** (the pigs) **What does the dog think happened to the pigs? Point to the part of the picture that helps you figure this out.** (He thinks the pigs squeezed through a gate. Children should point to the thought bubble.)

- **Page 6** **What does the dog think happened to the sheep? How do you know?** (He thinks they jumped over the fence. You can see it in the thought bubble.)

- **Page 7** **What picture clues tell that there should be cows here? What does the dog say?** (A barn, a milk can, and a pail of spilled milk are clues that it is the cows' place. The dog asks if the cows went away and if they will come back.) **What do you think will happen next?** (Children's predictions will vary.)

- **Page 8** **Where were all the animals? How do you know?** (They made a birthday party for the dog. They have a birthday cake, party hats, and a "Happy Birthday" banner.)

Reading Strategies

If... a child stumbles over the sentence patterns,	**Then...** reread the story in a shared reading. Read the first pages aloud, then be silent on selected words, and allow the child to finish reading the last page or two by himself or herself.
If... a child has trouble using context clues to identify the missing animals,	**Then...** use **Model Your Thinking** below.

Model Your Thinking

 Comprehension Skill: Context Clues

 Think ALOUD

In this book a dog searches for his animal friends. The pictures give clues about which animals are missing. On page 2, there is a picture of a feed sack with a hen on it. That tells me that the animals that live in this yard are probably hens. Another clue is the thought balloon. A thought balloon shows what a character is thinking. The dog's thought balloon shows hens running out of the yard. So I can guess that the dog thinks the hens ran away. The last clue is the picture of hens in the sentences. All these clues tell me that the missing animals are hens. If I keep looking for picture clues, I will be able to name all the missing animals.

After Reading

Revisiting the Text

Comprehension Have children use the Sequence Chart on page 139 to show the sequence of events in the book. Children can use context clues and then draw a picture of the animal the dog is looking for in each box. Make sure children follow the order of the animals in the book.

1B

Tex Has an Itch

by Nat Gabriel
Leveled Reader 1B
Genre: Fantasy
Level: Easy/Average

Summary

Tex, a cactus, has an itch. He wonders whether Horse or Bob will help, but they don't. Then Bird finally comes down to help.

Leveled Reader Practice

After children have read *Tex Has an Itch*, use Leveled Reader practice page 142 to assess their understanding of the Leveled Reader and the target comprehension skill. Additional after reading activities are provided on page 13.

At a Glance

Links to the Student Edition

⊙ **Comprehension Skill:** Context Clues

Selection Vocabulary: *no, down, come*

Program Theme: The World Around Us
Unit Theme: Take a Closer Look

It's great when we can look to friends for help. And it's even better when they can give it!

Before Reading

Motivating the Reader
Building Background About an Itch

Ask children what an itch is. Have them pretend they have a terrible itch in the middle of their backs, where it's hard to reach. Invite a few children at a time to dramatize their itches silently for the others.

> What can you do for an itch? What if you can't reach it? What do you say when your itch gets scratched?

Then tell children they will be reading a story about a character who has an itch.

Preview and Predict

Have children scan the cover, text, and illustrations. Encourage them to use picture clues and familiar words to predict what the story is about. Prepare children for reading by saying:

> In this story, Tex has a problem. He has an itch! He wonders if someone will help him. Look through the book. Who might come to help Tex?

Point out selection vocabulary and other unfamiliar words that are important to understanding the book, such as *itch* and *will*.

During Reading

Guiding Comprehension

Use the following questions to support children as they read.

- **Page 2** What is Tex's problem? (Tex has an itch.)

- **Page 3** Who does Tex hope will help him? How do you know? (Tex hopes Horse will help him. There is a horse in the picture and the text says "Horse.")

- **Page 4** Does Horse help Tex? How do you know? (No. Horse runs right past Tex. You can see the horse's hoof prints on the ground. The text says he does not help, and Tex looks sad.)

- **Page 5** Point to the word *Bob*. How do you say this word? What sound is at the beginning? What sound is at the end? (Children should give the correct pronunciation of *Bob*.)

- **Page 5** What kind of animal is Bob? (a bear)

- **Page 6** Does Bob help Tex? How do you know? (No. The footprints mean he has run past Tex.)

- **Page 7** Where is Bird? What will Bird have to do in order to help? (Bird is flying in the sky. Bird will have to come down to help.)

- **Page 8** Does Bird help? How do you know? (Yes. Bird scratches Tex's itch. Tex looks happy. The words say, "Yes! Ahhh!")

Reading Strategies

If... a child has trouble retelling the story sequence,	Then... have him or her use the Sequence Chart on page 139. He or she can draw a picture for the story beginning and for each possible helper until the end. Then he or she can use the chart to retell the story.
If... a child stumbles when reading the additional words on page 7,	Then... read the words aloud and then have the child repeat the words after you.
If... a child has trouble using context clues to follow what is happening in the story,	Then... use **Model Your Thinking** below.

Model Your Thinking

Think ALOUD

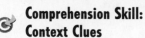
Comprehension Skill: Context Clues

This book has four characters. The words and the pictures give clues that tell us each character's name. On page 2, I can tell that the cactus is Tex, because it says, "Tex has an itch," and the cactus looks uncomfortable, as if it has an itch. On page 3 there is a horse in the picture and I see the name *Horse*. I see a bear on page 5. To figure out the bear's name, I look at the beginning, middle, and end sounds for this word. The bear's name is Bob. If I keep looking for picture and story clues, I will be able to figure out the characters' names and understand what is happening in the story.

After Reading

Revisiting the Text

Comprehension Reread the book together. As you read, encourage children to point out the context clues that help them figure out character names, what the problem in the story is, and how it gets solved.

2A
Come and Play

by Judy Nayer
Leveled Reader 2A
Genre: Realistic Story
Level: Easy

Summary

A child goes around the neighborhood calling for playmates. His arms get full as he collects a dog, a cat, a frog, a butterfly, and a bug. The weight of all these friends causes everyone to fall down.

Leveled Reader Practice

After children have read *Come and Play,* use Leveled Reader p ractice page 143 to assess their understanding of the Leveled Reader and the target comprehension skill. Additional after reading activities are provided on page 15.

At a Glance

Links to the Student Edition

⟳ **Comprehension Skill:** Cause and Effect

Selection Vocabulary: *all, play*

Program Theme: The World Around Us
Unit Theme: Take a Closer Look

Fun is all around us, if you know where to look.

Before Reading

Motivating the Reader
Building Background About All Fall Down

Invite one child to pretend she is holding a basket. Have her go from one child to another, and have each child add an imaginary animal to her basket. Encourage children to describe the basket's load. (Children should say the load is getting higher and heavier.) Then add a hippopotamus yourself and instruct the child carrying the basket to fall down.

Preview and Predict

Have children scan the cover, text, and illustrations. Encourage them to use picture clues and familiar words to predict what the story is about. Ask children what time of year the story takes place. (It is fall. There are colorful leaves on the ground.) Prepare children for reading by saying:

> In this story, a child wants someone to play with. Who does the child ask to come and play? What do you think will happen?

Point out selection vocabulary and other unfamiliar words that are important to understanding the book, such as *frog* and *butterfly.*

During Reading

Guiding Comprehension

Use the following questions to support children as they read.

- **Page 2** What **does the boy say to the dog?** (Come down, Dog!) **Why does the boy tell the dog to "come down"?** (The dog is up on a wall. The boy wants the dog to come down to play.)

- **Page 3** What animal **does the boy ask to join him? How do you know?** (He asks a cat. There is a cat in the picture and the words say, "Come down, Cat!") **What do you think will happen next? Why do you think that?** (The boy will ask more animals to come and play. Children should recognize the pattern of sentences and action.)

- **Page 4** What **do you think it feels like to hold a dog and a cat?** (It feels heavy. It might be hard to hold two animals.) **What will it feel like when the frog joins them?** (It will feel heavier and be more difficult to hold.)

- **Page 5** How many animals **does the child have now? How do you know?** (He has four animals, counting the butterfly. I can tell by counting the animal names on each page or by counting the animals in the picture.)

- **Pages 6–7** How many animals **does the boy have, including the bug? What do you think will happen? Why?** (Now he has five animals. They will fall down, because his arms are too full.)

- **Page 8** Read the sentence "We all fall down!" Put your fingers on *all* and *fall*. **What do you notice about these two words?** (They both have the letters *all* in them. They rhyme.)

- **Page 8** What happens on this page? (They all fall down.) **Why does this happen?** (The boy tried to carry too much.)

Reading Strategies

If... a child has difficulty recognizing the sentence patterns,	**Then...** reread the story in a shared reading. Read the first pages aloud, and then be silent on selected words as the child completes the pattern. Allow the child to finish reading the last few pages by himself or herself.
If... a child hesitates over the animal names,	**Then...** ask him or her to focus on the initial letter and sound of each name. Then suggest that the child use picture clues to help.
If... a child cannot recognize the cause-and-effect relationship in the story,	**Then...** use **Model Your Thinking** below.

Model Your Thinking

Comprehension Skill: Cause and Effect

The words and pictures help me know what is happening in the story. First, the boy takes the dog in his arms. Then, he picks up the cat. I want to read on to see what happens to the boy. He keeps picking up more animals. At the end of the story, everyone falls down. I ask myself, "Why does this happen?" I know that carrying this many animals is heavy, so I think they all fall down because they're too much for the boy to carry.

After Reading

Revisiting the Text

Comprehension Ask a volunteer to retell the story in his or her own words. Then ask children why they think the boy and the animals fell down. Record their answers on the chalkboard under the heading, *Why They All Fell Down.* Have children use the Sequence Chart on page 139 to draw what happened.

2B
Paper Fun

by Annie Temple
Leveled Reader 2B
Genre: Realistic Story
Level: Easy/Average

Summary

A boy complains that he cannot find his plane, his boat, or his hat. His older sister makes each one out of paper for him. But the boy still isn't happy, because now he can't see his sister. The hat she made for him is too big!

Leveled Reader Practice

After children have read *Paper Fun,* use Leveled Reader practice page 144 to assess their understanding of the Leveled Reader and the target comprehension skill. Additional after reading activities are provided on page 17.

At a Glance

Links to the Student Edition

☞ **Comprehension Skill:** Cause and Effect

Selection Vocabulary: *make, are, find*

Program Theme: The World Around Us
Unit Theme: Take a Closer Look

When you examine a problem carefully, you sometimes find the solution is right in front of your eyes.

Before Reading

Motivating the Reader
Building Background About Making Things with Paper

Give each child a piece of paper and invite the children to make something with the paper. Tell them they can cut, fold, and glue it. Have children share their creations. Then tell them they will read a story about having fun with paper.

Preview and Predict

Have children scan the cover, text, and illustrations. Encourage them to use picture clues and familiar words to predict what the story is about. Prepare children for reading by saying:

> Where on each page are the words in this book? How can you tell who is speaking? Let's read and find out what the children say and do.

Point out selection vocabulary and other unfamiliar words that are important to understanding the book, such as *can, not,* and *happy.*

During Reading

Guiding Comprehension

Use the following questions to support children as they read.

- **Page 2** *What can't the boy find? How do you know?* (He cannot find his toy plane. There is a picture of a plane, and the words say he cannot find his plane.)

- **Page 3** *What does his sister do?* (She tells him she will make a paper plane for him.) *How is the paper plane different from the boy's toy plane?* (It is a different shape from the toy plane. It is made of paper.)

- **Page 4** *What can't the boy find? How do you know?* (He cannot find his toy boat. There is a picture of a boat, and the words say he cannot find his boat.)

- **Pages 4–5** *Look at these two boats. How are the two boats alike? How are they different?* (The boats both have a sail, but they are different colors and different shapes. They are also made out of different things.) *Are the words under each boat the same? How do you know?* (The words are the same—boat. They show the same letters in the same order.)

- **Page 6** *What can't the boy find? How do you know?* (He cannot find his hat. There is a picture of a hat, and the words say he cannot find his hat.)

- **Page 8** *Why is the boy not happy?* (He is not happy because he cannot see his sister. The paper hat is too big, and it covers his eyes.)

Ongoing Assessment

Reading Strategies

If... a child seems confused by the different format on page 8,	Then... remind the child to read from top to bottom using the speech balloon "pointers" to tell who is talking.
If... a child quickly learns the sentence pattern and reads successive pages with growing confidence,	Then... praise him or her for recognizing sentence patterns.
If... a child cannot recognize cause-and-effect relationships,	Then... use **Model Your Thinking** below.

Model Your Thinking

 Comprehension Skill: Cause and Effect

In this story, the girl makes a paper plane, boat, and hat for the boy. At the end, the boy says he is not happy. He cannot see his sister! I ask myself, "Why can't he see? What is the cause of the problem?" I look at the boy's paper hat. It is covering his eyes. The hat is too big.

After Reading

Revisiting the Text

Comprehension Have children use the T-chart on page 140. They can draw the toys the boy can't find on one side and the paper objects his sister makes on the other side. Discuss how each pair is alike and different. Then invite children to reread pages 7–8, tell what happened with the paper hat, and explain what the cause of the problem was.

3A
Who Went Up?

by Babs Bell Hajdusiewicz
Leveled Reader 3A
Genre: Animal Fantasy
Level: Easy

Summary

Three bugs are playing outside. One at a time, they fly up in the air. Each time, the reader has to guess which bug went up.

Leveled Reader Practice

After children have read *Who Went Up?*, use Leveled Reader practice page 145 to assess their understanding of the Leveled Reader and the target comprehension skill. Additional after reading activities are provided on page 19.

At a Glance

Links to the Student Edition

🎯 **Comprehension Skill:** Predicting

Selection Vocabulary: *went, did, me*

Program Theme: The World Around Us
Unit Theme: Take a Closer Look

Sometimes when we read, we have to take a closer look in order to understand what is going on. If we look closely, we can figure out which bug went up in the air.

Before Reading

Motivating the Reader
Building Background About Going Up

Tell children they will read a story about some characters who go up in the air. Ask:

> What are some things you know that can go up in the air? Pretend you are going up in the air. What could lift or take you up—the wind? a bird? a balloon? a plane? a bouncy pair of shoes?

Invite children to draw a fun picture of themselves going up in the air.

Preview and Predict

Have children scan the cover, text, and illustrations. Encourage them to use picture clues and familiar words to predict what the story is about. Prepare children for reading by saying:

> In this story, you are asked to figure out who went up in the air. Look through the book. What kinds of clues can you find? Read the story to find out who goes up and what makes them go up.

Point out selection vocabulary and other unfamiliar words that are important to understanding the book, such as *who, look,* and *up*.

During Reading

Guiding Comprehension

Use the following questions to support children as they read.

- **Page 2** Who are the characters in the story? What is each one doing? (A grasshopper holds an umbrella. A caterpillar kicks a soccer ball. A ladybug is blowing up a balloon.)

- **Page 3** Who do you think went up? How do you know? (The grasshopper went up. I can see his green legs and purple sneakers. Also, the grasshopper is the only bug missing from the picture.)

- **Page 4** Who is speaking? How can you tell? (The grasshopper is speaking. He is the only one on the page, so the word *I* means he is the one speaking.)

- **Page 4** What do you think made this bug go up? (If wind got under his umbrella, it would lift him up.)

- **Page 5** Who do you think went up? How do you know? (The caterpillar went up. He was playing with the soccer ball, and a foot is kicking the ball up. The grasshopper has already gone up, and the ladybug is still on the ground.)

- **Page 6** What made the caterpillar go up? (Someone kicked the soccer ball the caterpillar was holding.)

- **Page 7** Who do you think went up? How do you know? (The ladybug went up. She is red and has black shoes. She is the only bug that hasn't gone up yet.)

- **Page 8** What does the ladybug want you to do? (Look at her.)

- **Page 8** What made the ladybug go up? (A balloon filled with air.)

Reading Strategies

If... a child can't name or describe each bug easily,	Then... allow him or her to express a prediction by pointing to a bug on page 2.
If... a child can tell what causes each bug to go up,	Then... praise the child for figuring out why things happen.
If... a child has difficulty making accurate predictions,	Then... use **Model Your Thinking** below.

Model Your Thinking

Comprehension Skill: Predicting

In this book, I have to figure out which bug went up. So I look for clues that will help me figure out who went up and how the bug went up. On page 3, I see hightop sneakers going up, and part of a green bug's body. When I look at page 2, I see that the green bug wearing hightops is the grasshopper. He also holds an umbrella. It looks like his legs and body going up on page 3. Since he was holding an umbrella, it must be what carried him up. If I keep looking at picture clues and remember what each bug was doing, I will be able to figure out which bug goes up.

After Reading

Revisiting the Text

Comprehension Ask children to reread the book and observe which bug was first, second, and third to go up. Invite children to tell the clues they used to figure out which bug went up each time. Then have children illustrate each bug going up in order.

3B
Go Away, Bugs!

by Sharon Fear
Leveled Reader 3B
Genre: Informational Article
Level: Easy/Average

Summary

The author warns bugs to go away—
they were seen by a bird that might eat
them. Questions and answers reveal
that what looks like a stick, bark, and a
leaf are really bugs hiding.

Leveled Reader Practice

After children have read *Go Away,
Bugs!*, use Leveled Reader practice
page 146 to assess their understanding
of the Leveled Reader and the target
comprehension skill. Additional after
reading activities are provided on
page 21.

At a Glance

Links to the Student Edition

Comprehension Skill: Predicting

Selection Vocabulary: *saw, walk*

**Program Theme: The World Around Us
Unit Theme: Take a Closer Look**

Taking a closer look can reveal some amazing
surprises. Bugs have disguises that help
them hide.

Before Reading

Motivating the Reader
Build Background About Bugs

Ask children to name and describe different
bugs they have seen. Encourage them to give
details of the bug's size, shape, and color, and to
tell what was special about it. Show children
pictures of different types of bugs. Invite
children to make a drawing of a bug that
interests them. Then tell them that they will
read about some very surprising bugs.

Preview and Predict

Have children scan the cover, text, and
illustrations. Encourage them to use picture
clues and familiar words to predict what the
story is about. Prepare children for reading
by saying:

> This book shows and tells about some
> interesting bugs. As you read, find out
> what is special about these bugs.

As they read, have children pause after each
question to answer it and predict what they
might see on the next page. Point out selection
vocabulary and other unfamiliar words that are
important to understanding the book, such as
stick, bark, leaf, and *hop.*

During Reading

Guiding Comprehension

Use the following questions to support children as they read.

- **Page 2 Why should the bugs go away?** (The bird is eating a bug. It might eat the other bugs too.)

- **Page 3 Do you see something else besides a stick? What do you see?** (The stick could be a bug. It has legs and feelers.)

- **Page 4** Point to the bug. **Is this a stick? How can you tell?** (No, it is a bug. I can see the bug's body and its legs. The words say it can walk and that it is a bug.)

- **Page 5 Do you think this is bark? What do you think it is?** (It could be a bug. I can see feelers and the wings don't look exactly like the tree bark. The bug on the other page was hiding, so I think this is a bug too.)

- **Page 7 Is that a leaf?** (No, it is a bug. It has wings that look like a leaf. All the other bugs look like something else.) **What do you think you will see on the next page?** (I will see this bug moving.)

- **Page 8 What can this bug do?** (It can hop away.)

- **Page 8 Do you think it is a good thing for a bug to look like a stick, a piece of bark, or a leaf? Why or why not? Think about what you read on the first page.** (Yes, it helps bugs hide so a bird won't find them and eat them.)

Ongoing Assessment

Reading Strategies

If... a child has difficulty pronouncing the final -ck in *stick*,	**Then...** say and write similar words, such as *sick* and *stuck*.
If... a child recognizes the bugs,	**Then...** praise him or her for identifying the sentence pattern and paying attention to the illustrations.
If... a child has difficulty making accurate predictions,	**Then...** use **Model Your Thinking** below.

Model Your Thinking

Comprehension Skill: Predicting

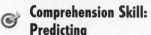

Think ALOUD

This book asks questions about what I see. On page 3, it asks, "Is that a stick?" I look for clues to help me answer this question. I see in the picture that the stick has legs and feelers like a bug. I see pictures of bugs and the word *bugs* on page 2. I think this "stick" is really a bug. I read on to see if I'm right. I find out on the next page that it is a bug. As I read, I see a pattern. Each time I am asked a question, it is about a bug that is hiding. The words and pictures give me clues that the story is about bugs that can hide by looking like parts of a tree.

After Reading

Revisiting the Text

Comprehension Ask children what clues they used to answer each question. Then have children discuss why they think the bugs have to hide by looking like parts of a tree. Invite children to invent additional pages to the story, illustrating them with real or imaginary bugs that blend into their surroundings.

4A
How Many on the Log?

by Sydnie Meltzer Kleinhenz
Leveled Reader 4A
Genre: Counting Book
Level: Easy

Summary

This simple counting book, in a question-and-answer format, is about frogs on a log. But something unexpected happens at the end when a cat scares all the frogs away!

Leveled Reader Practice

After children have read *How Many on the Log?*, use Leveled Reader practice page 147 to assess their understanding of the Leveled Reader and the target comprehension skill. Additional after reading activities are provided on page 23.

At a Glance

Links to the Student Edition

☞ **Comprehension Skill:** Setting

Selection Vocabulary: *how, many, on*

Program Theme: The World Around Us
Unit Theme: Take a Closer Look

In addition to reinforcing counting skills, the beautiful illustrations give the reader a closer look at the life cycle of frogs.

Before Reading

Motivating the Reader
Build Background About Frogs

Invite children to pretend they are frogs and ask them what they know about frogs.

> **What color are you? What do you look like? How do you move? What sounds do you make? Where do you live?**

Then tell children they will read a story about frogs.

Preview and Predict

Have children scan the cover, text, and illustrations. Encourage them to use picture clues and familiar words to predict where the story takes place and what it is about. Draw their attention to the marks at the end of the sentences, and help them describe the book's question-and-answer pattern. Encourage children to think about their own answer before reading the answer on each page.

Point out selection vocabulary and the number words, which are important to understanding the book.

During Reading

Guiding Comprehension

Use the following questions to support children as they read.

- **Page 2** Where does this story take place? How can you tell? (It takes place at the edge of a pond or river. There are plants, water, and a log in the picture.) What else can you see? (frog eggs, tadpoles, and some frogs)

- **Page 3** How many frogs are on the log? (There are two frogs on the log.) Which word on the page tells you how many frogs are on the log? (two)

- **Page 3** What do you think you will see on the next page? How do you know? (I will see three frogs on a log. First there was just one frog. Now there are two frogs. Three comes after two.) Ask similar questions until children recognize the pattern.

- **Page 6** Now how many frogs are on the log? Is there a pattern? (Now there are five frogs. Each time one more frog jumps on the log.)

- **Page 7** What do you think will happen next? (Predictions may vary. Possible answer: Another frog will jump onto the log. Maybe there will be so many frogs, they will fall off.)

- **Page 8** What happened? (A cat came along and scared the frogs away. They all jumped into the water!) Did this ending surprise you? (Answers will vary.)

Reading Strategies

If...	Then...
If... a child has difficulty with number words,	Then... help the child to count and write Arabic numerals on self-sticking notes to show the number of frogs.
If... a child calls attention to the rhyme of *frog* and *log*,	Then... praise the child for recognizing the phonogram *-og*. Encourage the child to think of other words that rhyme with *frog* and *log*.
If... a child has difficulty identifying the book's setting,	Then... use **Model Your Thinking** below.

Model Your Thinking

Think ALOUD

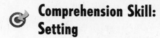
Comprehension Skill: Setting

As I read, I think about where and when a story takes place. Since this is a story about frogs, I know it must take place near water because frogs like water. The picture shows that there is water. It looks like a pond or a river. There are plants growing in the water and plants on the bank above the water. There is a log that is partly in the water. Maybe the pond or river is in the woods. I also can see frog eggs and tadpoles, so I know it must take place during the spring or summer, when new frogs are born.

After Reading

Revisiting the Text

Comprehension Have children reread the story, paying attention to the different elements that appear in the pictures on each page. Have volunteers hold up the book, pointing to and describing the story's setting. Invite children to describe their own experiences walking in nature, telling what they saw.

4B

With the Fish

by Susan McCloskey
Leveled Reader 4B
Genre: Realistic Story
Level: Easy/Average

Summary
This story takes place at an aquarium, where different children spot brightly colored fish hiding among plants in the tanks.

Leveled Reader Practice
After children have read *With the Fish*, use Leveled Reader practice page 148 to assess their understanding of the Leveled Reader and the target comprehension skill. Additional after reading activities are provided on page 25.

At a Glance

Links to the Student Edition
Comprehension Skill: Setting

Selection Vocabulary: *happy, they, why*

Program Theme: The World Around Us
Unit Theme: Take a Closer Look

Sometimes things aren't what they seem to be, and we have to take a closer look. If we look closely at a fish tank, we may see interesting fish hiding.

Before Reading

Motivating the Reader
Build Background About Fish

Ask children about the fish they have seen and where they have seen them. If necessary, explain that one place they might see fish is in an aquarium, which is a kind of zoo for fish. Talk about why people would want to see fish in an aquarium.

Preview and Predict

Have children scan the cover, text, and illustrations. Encourage them to use picture clues and familiar words to predict where the story happens and what it is about. Prepare children for reading by saying:

> Where do you think this story takes place? What clues help you figure it out? In this story, the children are happy. This word is repeated on many pages. As you read, find out what the children see that makes them happy.

Point out selection vocabulary and other unfamiliar words that are important to understanding the book, such as the color words *green, yellow, red,* and *purple.*

During Reading

Guiding Comprehension

Use the following questions to support children as they read.

- **Page 2** **Where is Pam? How can you tell?** (Pam is standing outside a big fish tank. Maybe she's at an aquarium. I can see that she is looking through glass at some fish.)

- **Pages 2–3** **Can you see the green fish? Point out the green fish. What else do you see in the tank?** (Yes, the green fish is hiding in the plants. There also are plants with long, wavy leaves in the tank.)

- **Page 3** Point to the word *they*. **What is this word?** (they) **What does it mean?** (*They* means the green fish.)

- **Page 4** **What did Tim see? How do you know? Put your finger under the word** *yellow*. (Tim saw yellow fish. I see the words *yellow fish,* and I see fish that are yellow.)

- **Page 5** **Why do the fish in this picture look bigger now?** (It's the same fish, but we are seeing them closer up.)

- **Page 6** **What did Max and Rick see? How do you know?** (Max and Rick saw red fish. The words say they saw red fish, and I can see red fish in the picture.)

- **Page 7** **What do the fish look like? What else is in the tank?** (The fish are long and thin like snakes, and they have lots of teeth. There are feathery plants in the tank too.)

- **Page 8** **What did Jan see? What else do you see?** (Jan saw purple fish. The fish have long, funny noses and big eyes. There are long blades of grass in the tank.)

- **Page 8** **Which word on this page tells about a feeling?** (happy) **Why are the children happy?** (They like seeing the fish.)

Reading Strategies

If... a child has trouble with the words that name colors,	**Then...** help the child use the illustrations to associate the color with its word name.
If... a child has trouble identifying the book's setting,	**Then...** use **Model Your Thinking** below.

Model Your Thinking

Think ALOUD

🗣 **Comprehension Skill: Setting**

As I read, I think about where the story takes place. One clue is the fish. It's a place where fish live, but the children can be right near them without getting wet. So I know the fish must be in tanks. The fish are in the water, and the children are looking through the glass walls of the tanks. There are plants in the tanks. Maybe each tank is made to be like the place where the fish in it come from. I have visited an aquarium where there were fish in tanks with rocks and plants, so I think this story takes place at an aquarium.

After Reading

Revisiting the Text

Comprehension Reread the book with children, reading each left-hand page aloud with them and pointing to each word with your finger. Then have the children read each right-hand page aloud by themselves. Have children use the Sequence Chart on page 139. Above the first box, write the sentence: "Pam saw green fish." Invite children to draw and color the fish in the box. For each succeeding story part, write part or all of a similar sentence, and then have children complete the sentence and illustrate it in the box.

5A
Jack and Jill

retold by Phoebe Marsh
Leveled Reader 5A
Genre: Rhyme
Level: Easy

Summary

Based on the familiar nursery rhyme, this book tells the story of Jack and Jill with a surprise ending. The bucket of water makes a great swimming pool for these tiny frogs.

Leveled Reader Practice

After children have read *Jack and Jill,* use Leveled Reader practice page 149 to assess their understanding of the Leveled Reader and the target comprehension skill. Additional after reading activities are provided on page 27.

At a Glance

Links to the Student Edition

↻ **Comprehension Skill:** Author's Purpose

Selection Vocabulary: *does, he, water*

Program Theme: The World Around Us
Unit Theme: Take a Closer Look

Readers take a closer look at a familiar nursery rhyme and find a surprise ending.

Before Reading

Motivating the Reader
Build Background About Wells

Explain to children that when people don't have running water in their homes, they have to go to a well with a pitcher or pail and carry water home. A well is a hole that goes deep into the earth and contains underground water. People have to operate a pump or pull a bucket on a rope to bring up water. Display the picture of the well on the book's back cover and/or a picture of an actual well. Call attention to the pail hanging above the hole in the cover picture. With the children, dramatize how you might let down the well bucket, fill it, pull it up, and pour the water into your own pail.

Preview and Predict

Have children scan the cover, text, and illustrations. Encourage them to use picture clues and familiar words to predict what the story is about. Prepare children for reading by saying:

> This book is a rhyme that you may know, but it has a different ending. As you read, listen for the rhymes. Which words rhyme? Read and watch to see what happens to Jack and Jill.

Point out selection vocabulary and other unfamiliar words that are important to understanding the book, such as *pail, crown,* and *tumbling.* Encourage children to use the story, letter/sound clues, and the pictures to figure out how to read these unfamiliar words and figure out what they mean.

During Reading

Guiding Comprehension

Use the following questions to support children as they read.

- **Pages 2–3** **Which characters in the picture are Jack and Jill? How do you know?** (Jack and Jill are the frogs. I know it's them because they are pulling a pail up the hill.) **Which words rhyme? How can you tell?** (*Jill* and *hill* rhyme. They have the same ending sound.)

- **Page 4** **What happened to Jack?** (Jack fell down the hill.)

- **Page 5** Point to the word *crown.* **What is this word? Look at the picture. Think of a word that rhymes with *down* that makes sense in this sentence.** (crown)

- **Page 5** **What did Jack break?** (his crown) **What rhyming words are on these two pages?** (*down* and *crown*)

- **Page 6** **What happened to Jill? How do you know?** (Jill fell down too. The words say "came tumbling after," and *tumbling* means the same as *falling*. In the picture Jill is falling down.)

- **Page 7** **What do you think Jack and Jill might do?** (Answers will vary.)

- **Page 8** **What do Jack and Jill do? Do you think they are enjoying themselves?** (They go swimming in the pail of water. Yes, they look happy, and it says, "They have fun!")

- **Page 8** **Were you surprised by the book's ending?** (Encourage well-supported answers.) **Is this a funny book or a sad book? How do you know?** (It is funny because it has a surprise ending that is funny.)

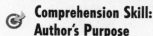

Ongoing Assessment

Reading Strategies

If... a child struggles with the text, reading word by word,	**Then...** read each sentence aloud with the child. Then have the child tell you its meaning in his or her own words.
If... a child already knew the rhyme and reads the text correctly,	**Then...** praise him or her for using prior knowledge *and* reading the text carefully.
If... a child has difficulty explaining the tone of the book,	**Then...** use **Model Your Thinking** below.

Model Your Thinking

🎯 **Comprehension Skill: Author's Purpose**

I know that there are many different kinds of books. Some are funny. Some are sad. Some tell about real life, and some are make-believe. Before I read, I look to see who the author is—the person who wrote the book. Then I look at the words and pictures to find out what the book will be like. The author's name is on the cover. Phoebe Marsh wrote the words for this book. Chris Demarest is the illustrator who drew the pictures for it. I know this story is make-believe because I see pictures of animals wearing clothes. I see the frogs fall down, but they don't look like they are badly hurt. This last picture shows them having fun, and I see the word *fun.* These clues tell me this is a funny story.

After Reading

Revisiting the Text

Comprehension Invite children to retell the story in their own words. Ask them to tell what they liked about the story and whether they found it funny or sad. Have them draw pictures to show their favorite part of the book.

5B

In and Out

by Dona R. McDuff
Leveled Reader 5B
Genre: Realistic Story
Level: Easy/Average

Summary

During the night, a raccoon wanders through the woods and into a shed to steal some food from a garbage can. When it goes into a cave to enjoy its meal, it is surprised to find a smelly skunk!

Leveled Reader Practice

After children have read *In and Out,* use Leveled Reader practice page 150 to assess their understanding of the Leveled Reader and the target comprehension skill. Additional after reading activities are provided on page 29.

At a Glance

Links to the Student Edition

Comprehension Skill: Author's Purpose

Selection Vocabulary: *this, into*

Program Theme: The World Around Us
Unit Theme: Take a Closer Look

Take a closer look at the world as it appears to a raccoon searching for food in the middle of the night.

Before Reading

Motivating the Reader
Build Background About Raccoons

Display a photograph of a raccoon or the cover of the book, and ask children to name the animal and describe it. Encourage children who have seen raccoons to share their experiences. Tell students that raccoons are usually active at night and that they are known for being very curious animals.

Preview and Predict

Have children scan the cover, text, and illustrations. Encourage them to use picture clues and familiar words to predict what the story is about. Prepare children for reading by saying:

> In this book, you will follow a raccoon into different places. Look at the pictures and the words to find out where the raccoon goes and what it does.

Point out selection vocabulary and other unfamiliar words that are important to understanding the book, such as *garden* and *shed.*

During Reading

Guiding Comprehension

Use the following questions to support children as they read.

- **Page 2** Do you think this book will tell about things that a real raccoon would *do* or a make-believe raccoon? How do you know? (It looks like a real raccoon doing things a real raccoon would do. It doesn't talk or wear clothes like a make-believe raccoon might.)

- **Pages 2–3** What time of day is it? How do you know? (It is late at night. It is dark, and the moon is shining.) What is the raccoon doing? (It is walking through a log and into a tree.)

- **Pages 2–3** Which words on these pages name the things the raccoon climbs into? (log, tree)

- **Page 4** Point to the word *garden*. What is this word? Look at the picture and think about the beginning sound of this word. (garden)

- **Page 5** Where does the raccoon go now? Where do you think the raccoon is—the city or the country? How do you know? (The raccoon goes into a shed. It must be the country since it has trees and a garden.)

- **Page 6** What is the raccoon doing? How do you know? (The raccoon is looking in the garbage can for food. It has found an ear of corn.)

- **Page 7** Where does the raccoon go? (into a cave)

- **Page 8** What happens in the cave? Why does this happen? (The raccoon sees a skunk in the cave. The raccoon runs away from the skunk. The skunk could spray the raccoon with a bad smell that the raccoon probably wouldn't like.)

Reading Strategies

If... a child is not familiar with the word *into*,	**Then...** dramatize it with classroom objects. Move your hand into a bag or box and then out, saying the words *into* and *out*. Dramatize going *into* and *out of* the classroom. Then read the story together.
If... a child correctly reads unfamiliar words, using sound–letter relationships and picture clues,	**Then...** praise him or her for using good decoding skills.
If... a child has difficulty telling what the story is like,	**Then...** use **Model Your Thinking** below.

Model Your Thinking

Comprehension Skill: Author's Purpose

As I look at the pictures in this book I see the raccoon walking and climbing through the woods and into a shed. I see that the raccoon is curious and hungry. It pokes into everything and takes an ear of corn from a garbage can. Finally the raccoon bumps into a skunk and runs away. I think the author, Dona McDuff, wrote this book to show readers things that real raccoons do. I like learning about raccoons, and I think the ending is funny.

After Reading

Revisiting the Text

Comprehension Reread the story with the children. Have children tell what they have learned about raccoons. Draw a word web on the chalkboard, and write *Raccoon* in the center. Write the different things children learned at the ends of the spokes.

6A
Stop! Eat!

by Cass Hollander
Leveled Reader 6A
Genre: Realistic Fiction
Level: Easy

Summary

A mother armadillo takes her children on a nighttime prowl for food. After eating some bugs and leaves, the armadillos find a backpack at a campground. But before they have a chance to eat what's inside, some campers surprise them.

Leveled Reader Practice

After children have read *Stop! Eat!*, use Leveled Reader practice page 151 to assess their understanding of the Leveled Reader and the target comprehension skill. Additional after reading activities are provided on page 31.

At a Glance

Links to the Student Edition

Comprehension Skill: Cause and Effect

Selection Vocabulary: *stop, eat*

Program Theme: The World Around Us
Unit Theme: Take a Closer Look

A mother armadillo helps her babies take a closer look at the world and find things to eat.

Before Reading

Motivating the Reader
Build Background About Armadillos

Show pictures and share simple facts about armadillos, such as their size, where they live, what they eat, and other interesting habits they have. Invite students to tell how armadillos are like and unlike other animals they know about. Encourage children to think about what a mother armadillo and her babies might be doing prowling about at night.

Preview and Predict

Have children scan the cover, text, and illustrations. Encourage them to use picture clues and familiar words to predict what the story is about. Prepare children for reading by saying:

Who do you think says, "Stop! Eat!"?
Why would the character say that?
Read to find out what happens to the armadillos during their night out.

Point out selection vocabulary and other unfamiliar words that are important to understanding the book, such as *leaves*.

During Reading

⬤ Guiding Comprehension

Use the following questions to support children as they read.

- **Pages 2–3** **What time of day is it? How do you know?** (It is night. It is dark, and the moon and stars are shining.) **Who is speaking? How do you know?** (The mother armadillo is speaking. She is telling her babies to stop and eat the bugs.)

- **Page 4** **Have you seen these words before? Where have you seen these words?** (Yes. They are on page 2 also.)

- **Pages 4–5** **What happens next?** (The mother armadillo tells her babies to eat some leaves.)

- **Page 6** **What is happening now?** (The armadillos find a backpack. The mother is sniffing it.) **Where do you think this backpack came from? How do you know?** (It probably belongs to some campers. There is a tent in the picture.)

- **Page 7** **What are the baby armadillos doing?** (They are starting to eat the food in the backpack.)

- **Page 8** **Who do you think says "Stop!"?** (The family in the tent. They do not want the armadillos to eat their food.) **What do you think the armadillos will do now?** (They will run away and hide.) **How would you feel if you found armadillos sniffing your backpack?** (Possible answers: I would be mad. I would think it was funny. I would be very surprised.)

- **Page 8** **What does this book tell you about armadillos?** (Armadillos eat bugs and leaves. They will also eat food people leave out. Mother armadillos teach their babies what to eat.)

Reading Strategies

If... a child reads exclamatory sentences without emphasis,	**Then...** model appropriate intonation for him or her. Then have the child read the story again with expression.
If... a child calls attention to the repetition of *stop* and *eat*,	**Then...** praise him or her for paying attention to sentence patterns.
If... a child cannot recognize cause-and-effect relationships,	**Then...** use **Model Your Thinking** below.

Model Your Thinking

 Comprehension Skill: Cause and Effect

As I read, I think about what happens in the story and why those things happen. On page 2, what happens is that the mother armadillo says to her babies, "Stop! Eat!" On page 3, she and her babies eat some bugs. I ask myself why they do this. I think it is because they are hungry. I also think the mother armadillo is teaching her babies how to hunt for food. Thinking about what happens and why it happens helps me better understand the story.

After Reading

Revisiting the Text

Comprehension Organize the children into four groups. Have the first three groups read aloud two pages each and explain why the armadillos stop each time. Have the last group read page 8 aloud and explain who says, "Stop!" and why. Have each group draw a picture about their assigned pages. Help them write a caption telling what happens in it and why it happens.

6B

Night Songs

by Linda Yoshizawa
Leveled Reader 6B
Genre: Non-rhyming Poem
Level: Easy/Average

Summary

A boy sits by his open bedroom window listening to the night songs sung by owls, frogs, and his parents.

Leveled Reader Practice

After children have read *Night Songs,* use Leveled Reader practice page 152 to assess their understanding of the Leveled Reader and the target comprehension skill. Additional after reading activities are provided on page 33.

At a Glance

Links to the Student Edition

Comprehension Skill: Cause and Effect

Selection Vocabulary: *by, them, sing*

Program Theme: The World Around Us
Unit Theme: Take a Closer Look

Taking a closer look at the world around us doesn't always involve our eyes. Sometimes we have to *listen* more closely.

Before Reading

Motivating the Reader
Build Background About Night Sounds

Have children close their eyes and sit very still for a minute or two, listening for sounds. Ask children to share the sounds they heard. Ask them if they know what was making each sound. Remind children that the world is seldom silent. Nature has many sounds, even at night. Then ask children to share some familiar night sounds.

Preview and Predict

Have children scan the cover, text, and illustrations. Encourage them to use picture clues and familiar words to predict what the story is about. Prepare children for reading by saying:

> The title of this book is Night Songs. Look at the words and pictures. What "songs" do you think you can hear at night? Read to find out what night songs are and who sings them.

Point out selection vocabulary and other unfamiliar words that are important to understanding the book, such as *night, owls, hears,* and *do.*

During Reading

Guiding Comprehension

Use the following questions to support children as they read.

- **Pages 2–3** *What time of day is it? How can you tell?* (It is nighttime. It is dark and the moon is out.) *Where is this place? What clues help you figure this out?* (It is in the country. I see animals, a farm house, and a barn. There are no other houses nearby.)

- **Page 3** *Who is singing?* (Owls are singing.) *What song might an owl sing?* (Hoot! Hoot!)

- **Pages 4–5** *What other animals sing at night? Where do you think they live?* (Frogs sing at night. They live in a pond.) *What song might a frog sing?* (Ribbit! Ribbit!)

- **Pages 6–7** *Who else is singing at night?* (A mother and father are singing.)

- **Page 8** *Who is speaking? How do you know?* (The boy is speaking. The word *I* is a clue that these are the boy's words. He looks like he is listening.)

- **Page 8** *Why is the boy leaning out an open window?* (He does this so he can hear the night songs.) *Why is the boy smiling?* (He smiles because he likes the songs he hears.)

Reading Strategies

If... a child hesitates when reading a word, but then reads it correctly,

Then... ask the child how he or she knew what the word was. This will help the child build a greater awareness of the fix-up strategies he or she uses when reading.

If... a child cannot explain the effects of the night songs on the boy,

Then... use **Model Your Thinking** below.

Model Your Thinking

 Comprehension Skill: Cause and Effect

Think ALOUD

As I read, I pay attention to what happens in the book and why these things happen. This book tells about the different songs, or sounds, a boy hears at night. On page 8, I see the boy is leaning out an open window and is smiling. I ask myself, "Why is he doing this? What is making him smile?" I know I can hear sounds outdoors better if a window is open, so I think he leans out the window so he can hear better. On pages 2 through 7, I read about all of the different night songs that he hears. He is probably smiling because he likes the songs owls, frogs, and his parents sing.

After Reading

Revisiting the Text

Comprehension Use the T-Chart on page 140. At the top of the left column, write: *Whose night songs does the boy hear?* At the top of the right column write: *What sound does this night song have?* Have pairs reread the book together and write words or draw pictures to complete the chart. Invite children to talk about sounds they hear that make them feel happy like the boy in the story.

7A
Goal!

by Rory Thomas
Leveled Reader 7A
Genre: Realistic Story
Level: Easy

Summary

Kit and Tim are getting ready for a soccer game. Kit cannot do some things by herself, so she asks Tim for help. However, the tables are turned in the end when Kim scores a goal off Tim, the goalie.

Leveled Reader Practice

After children have read *Goal!,* use Leveled Reader practice page 153 to assess their understanding of the Leveled Reader and the target comprehension skill. Additional after reading activities are provided on page 35.

At a Glance

Links to the Student Edition

◉ **Comprehension Skill:** Compare and Contrast

Selection Vocabulary: *help, said*

Program Theme: Learning and Working
Unit Theme: Let's Learn Together

Asking for help from others, as well as giving help to others, are important ways we can learn together.

Before Reading

Motivating the Reader
Build Background About Soccer

Ask children if they have ever played or watched a soccer game. Have them share what they know about the game, including the equipment used and the rules of play. Make sure students understand how teams score points and what goalies do to try to prevent opponents from scoring. Invite volunteers to demonstrate moving a ball using their feet. Then tell children they will read a story about children playing soccer.

Preview and Predict

Have children scan the cover, text, and illustrations. Encourage them to use picture clues and familiar words to predict what the story is about. Prepare children for reading by saying:

> In this book, one child asks for and gets help from another child. Read the story and find out what kinds of help she needs. Does she always need help?

Point out selection vocabulary and other unfamiliar words that are important to understanding the book, such as *get* and *goal.*

During Reading

Guiding Comprehension

Use the following questions to support children as they read.

- **Page 2** Who is asking for help? How do you know? (The girl Kit is asking for help. The picture shows she can't reach the ball. The words *said Kit* tell who is saying the words.)

- **Page 3** Does Tim help Kit? How do you know? (Yes. Tim reaches for the ball, and he says, "I can get it.")

- **Page 4** What does Kit need help with? Why might she need help? (Kit needs help putting on shin guards. Maybe Tim has played more soccer and can do it more easily.)

- **Page 5** What does Tim mean when he says, "I can get it"? (Tim means that he can take care of it.)

- **Pages 6–7** Now what does Kit need help with? Do you think she will be a good soccer player? Why or why not? (Kit needs help with tying her shoelaces. I think she won't be a very good soccer player because she seems to need help with everything.)

- **Page 8** Are Kit and Tim playing on the same team? How do you know? (No. Tim is the goalie who tries to keep Kit's team from scoring. Kit kicks the ball past Tim. They are wearing different clothes.)

- **Page 8** What has happened? Did you think this would happen? (Tim couldn't stop the ball, and Kit kicked it in for a goal. I did not think this would happen because Kit needed so much help from Tim. I was surprised that she could play soccer so well.)

- **Page 8** What are some ways that Kit and Tim are alike? (They both are blonde. They are about the same age. They like to play soccer.) What are some ways that Kit and Tim are different? (They wear different clothes and play on different teams. Kit often asks for help, and Tim often helps Kit. Tim is taller than Kit.)

Reading Strategies

If... a child hesitates at the quotation marks,	Then... remind him or her that all the words inside the marks are words the speaker says.
If... a child doesn't understand that Kit and Tim play on different teams,	Then... have the child look at the clothing on the players on page 6. Talk with a child about how points are scored in soccer.
If... a child has difficulty comparing and contrasting characters in the book,	Then... use **Model Your Thinking** below.

Model Your Thinking

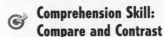 **Comprehension Skill: Compare and Contrast**

As I read about Kit and Tim, I look to see how they are alike, or the same, and how they are different. They both are blonde. They look the same age. They both like to play soccer. These are ways they are both alike. But Kit is a girl, and Tim is a boy. Tim also is taller than Kit. That's why he was able to reach the ball in the tree. They wear different clothes and play on different teams. These are ways they are different. Thinking about how Kit and Tim are alike and different helps me understand them better.

After Reading

Revisiting the Text

Comprehension Ask children to reread the book, noticing all the ways that Kit and Tim are alike and different. Use the T-Chart on page 140 to organize children's ideas. Have children draw or write items in columns marked *Alike* and *Different*. Then ask children to make statements about ways Kit and Tim are alike or different, using the information in the chart.

7B
This Means Stop

by Myka-Lynne Sokoloff
Leveled Reader 7B
Genre: Realistic Story
Level: Easy/Average

Summary

A woman and her son observe the traffic at a busy intersection. Watching the crossing guard's signals, they pay attention to the cars crossing the intersection. At last, they can cross the street. Why? The guard says so!

Leveled Reader Practice

After children have read *This Means Stop,* use Leveled Reader practice page 154 to assess their understanding of the Leveled Reader and the target comprehension skill. Additional after reading activities are provided on page 37.

At a Glance

Links to the Student Edition

⟳ **Comprehension Skill:** Compare and Contrast

Selection Vocabulary: *now, who, so*

Program Theme: Learning and Working
Unit Theme: Let's Learn Together

A mother and son learn the importance of traffic rules. When both drivers and pedestrians follow the crossing guard's signals, everyone gets where they need to go safely.

Before Reading

Motivating the Reader
Build Background About Traffic Signals

Tell children they will read about traffic signals, and invite them to act out a traffic scene. One child can pretend he or she is a crossing guard. The other children can be pedestrians and motorists. Have the crossing guard direct the traffic using hand signals. After children act out the scene, discuss how they knew what the crossing guard was telling them to do.

Preview and Predict

Have children scan the cover, text, and illustrations. Encourage them to use picture clues and familiar words to predict what the story is about. Prepare children for reading by asking:

> Who do you think is speaking? What are the boy and the mother doing? What is the person in the middle of the street doing? As you read, pay attention to the crossing guard's hands and face.

Point out selection vocabulary and other unfamiliar words that are important to understanding the book, such as *stop, go, turn,* and *slow.*

During Reading

● Guiding Comprehension

Use the following questions to support children as they read.

- **Page 2** *Where does this story take place?* (The story is set at a busy street crossing.) **How do the woman and the boy know they have to stop?** (The guard's hand is telling them to stop. Also, the stop sign tells them they have to stop.)

- **Page 3** *What signal does the crossing guard make now? What do you think it means?* (She points, which lets the taxi driver know he can go through the intersection.)

- **Page 3** *How are these two sentences alike?* (They both have the phrase "can go now.") **How are they different?** (The first sentence is a question. The second sentence tells the answer to the question.)

- **Page 4** *What signal does the guard make now? How do you know?* (The guard signals to the ice cream truck that it can turn, and points the way. The words say the truck can turn now.)

- **Page 4** Point to *turn*. **What does this word mean? What is the truck doing?** (It means "to go around a corner." The truck is turning to drive on a new street.)

- **Page 5** *What signal does the guard make now? How do you know?* (She signals two cars to slow down. She spreads her hands, which means "Slow down." Also the words say "They can go so slow.")

- **Page 6** *Who can go now?* (The woman and the boy can go now.)

- **Page 8** *How does the story end?* (The woman and the boy cross the street safely. The boy waves to the guard.)

Reading Strategies

If... a child recognizes that *go*, *so*, and *slow* rhyme,	**Then...** praise him or her for paying attention to the ending sounds of the words.
If... a child has difficulty comparing and contrasting events in the book,	**Then...** use **Model Your Thinking** below.

Model Your Thinking

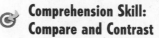 **Comprehension Skill: Compare and Contrast**

Think ALOUD

One way I can better understand this book is to look at how things are alike and different. *Alike* means the same. *Different* means not the same. In this book, the crossing guard uses her hands to tell people what to do. These are signals. As I read the words and look at the pictures I can figure out what the signal means. On page 2, the guard holds up her hand. This signal means stop. On page 3, I see the guard point forward. She is telling the drivers they can go forward now. As I keep reading, I pay attention to the guard's hands. Page 6 shows the same stop signal as page 2. The guard is stopping the cars. Page 7 shows the same signal as page 3. The guard is telling the mother and the boy to go across the street. Paying attention to signals that are the same and different helps me understand what is happening.

After reading

Revisiting the Text

Comprehension Have pairs reread the story together and look at the hand signals the crossing guard uses. Have them draw pictures of each signal and write what it means. Have students compare and contrast their pictures, grouping like pictures together.

8A

Hic! Hic! Hic!

by Deborah Eaton
Leveled Reader 8A
Genre: Animal Fantasy
Level: Easy

Summary

Beaver, Mole, and Raccoon find holes in a leaf, a book, a map, and a curtain in the classroom. While they are trying to figure out who made the holes, they hear, "Hic! Hic! Hic!" from behind a curtain. Out pops a hiccuping Pat the Porcupine!

Leveled Reader Practice

After children have read *Hic! Hic! Hic!*, use Leveled Reader practice page 155 to assess their understanding of the Leveled Reader and the target comprehension skill. Additional after reading activities are provided on page 39.

At a Glance

Links to the Student Edition

↻ **Comprehension Skill:** Drawing Conclusions

Selection Vocabulary: *some, too*

Program Theme: Learning and Working
Unit Theme: Let's Learn Together

It's always easier to solve a mystery with the help of others.

Before Reading

Motivating the Reader
Build Background About Mysteries

Present children with some simple mysteries to solve: a piece of paper with three holes punched in the side, a rag with paint on it, and a gardening glove with dirt on it. Ask children to examine these objects and tell what happened to each object. Ask prompting questions as needed to help them figure out that a paper punch made the holes, the rag was used to clean paint brushes, and the glove was used to garden. Discuss what clues help them solve each mystery.

Preview and Predict

Have children scan the cover, text, and illustrations. Encourage them to use picture clues and familiar words to predict what the story is about. Prepare children for reading by saying:

> **Who are the characters in this book? What is strange about the things they are looking at? Read to find out who made the holes.**

Point out selection vocabulary and other unfamiliar words that are important to understanding the book, such as *has, holes, did,* and *hiccups.*

During Reading

Guiding Comprehension

Use the following questions to support children as they read.

- **Pages 2–3** *Who are the characters in this book?* (The characters are a beaver, a mole, and a raccoon.) *What have they found?* (They have found holes in a leaf.) *What does the raccoon ask?* (The raccoon asks who made the holes in the leaf.)

- **Page 4** *What does the mole find?* (He finds holes in a book.)

- **Page 5** *Who finds more holes? How can you tell?* (The beaver finds more holes. I can see his tail sticking out from behind the map.) *Where does he find them?* (He finds them in a map.)

- **Page 5** *What question does each character ask?* (Who did this?)

- **Page 6** *Where do the animals find more holes?* (They find more holes in a curtain.)

- **Page 7** *In your own words, describe what is happening. How do you think the animals feel?* (The animals hear a noise: "Hic! Hic! Hic!" They look scared and confused. They don't know what is making the noise.)

- **Page 7** Point to the speech balloons. *What do these words show?* (They show the sounds that are coming from behind the curtain.) *Read these words. What do you think is making these sounds?* (Predictions will vary. Children may connect the sounds with hiccups and use picture clues to predict a hiccupping porcupine is making the sounds.)

- **Page 8** *Who was behind the curtain making noise?* (Pat the Porcupine was behind the curtain.) *How do you think he made the holes?* (He probably made the holes with his quills when he was bouncing around with the hiccups.)

Reading Strategies

If... a child hesitates when reading,	**Then...** ask the child to tell in his or her own words what is happening. Support the child in decoding the words. Encourage him or her to use picture clues and sentence patterns as well.
If... a child has difficulty drawing logical conclusions,	**Then...** use **Model Your Thinking** below.

Model Your Thinking

Think ALOUD

🎯 **Comprehension Skill: Drawing Conclusions**

As I read, I pay attention to word and picture clues to help me figure out more about the characters and what happens in the story. I also think about what I know from my own life. In this story, the characters have found holes in a leaf, a book, a map, and a curtain. They wonder who is making the holes. On page 8, I see Pat, a porcupine, has the hiccups. I know that porcupines have sharp quills on their bodies. I see that Pat bounces up when he hiccups. These clues help me figure out that it is Pat who is making the holes. His quills poke through things when Pat bounces against them.

After Reading

Revisiting the Text

Comprehension Use the Problem and Solution chart on page 137 to help children draw conclusions about the book. In the problem box, write: *Who made the holes?* Ask children to use clues from the book to figure out the answer. Have children write words and/or draw pictures to explain who made the holes and how the holes were made.

8B

Oh, Good!

by Judy Nayer
Leveled Reader 8B
Genre: Realistic Story
Level: Easy/Average

Summary

A girl decides to get rid of an old quilt, a book, and a number of other things. Her younger sister follows her around, collecting all the discarded items. The younger sister makes a little hideaway for herself with all the items. But when her older sister sees how much fun she is having in her hideaway, the younger sister decides to share everything with her.

Leveled Reader Practice

After children have read *Oh, Good!*, use Leveled Reader practice page 156 to assess their understanding of the Leveled Reader and the target comprehension skill. Additional after reading activities are provided on page 41.

At a Glance

Links to the Student Edition

Comprehension Skill: Drawing Conclusions

Selection Vocabulary: *want, good, for*

Program Theme: Learning and Working
Unit Theme: Let's Learn Together

A young girl learns that it's often more fun to share with others.

Before Reading

Motivating the Reader
Build Background About Sisters and Brothers

Prepare a large version of the T-Chart on page 140 on chart paper. Title the chart *Sisters and Brothers* and label the columns *Being Younger* and *Being Older.* Ask children if they have sisters and brothers and what it feels like to be the younger or the older child. Have them state some good things and some things that are hard about being a younger brother or sister, and write them on the chart. Do the same for older sisters and brothers. Children can mark the chart, circling things that are good about being younger or older with a red crayon, and circling things that are hard in purple.

Preview and Predict

Have children scan the cover, text, and illustrations. Encourage them to use picture clues and familiar words to predict what the story is about. Have a volunteer read the first two pages aloud. Help children use picture clues to identify which sister is saying each sentence. Suggest children read to find out what the two sisters are doing.

Point out selection vocabulary and other unfamiliar words that are important to understanding the book, such as *you* and *me*. Make sure children understand that the pictures in the sentences stand for a word. These words are printed below the pictures. Encourage them to look at the beginning and ending sounds of these words.

During Reading

Guiding Comprehension

Use the following questions to support children as they read.

- **Page 2** *Who is speaking? How do you know?* (The girl by the closet is speaking. She says "I do not want this quilt" and I see her getting rid of a quilt in the picture.)

- **Page 3** *Who do you think this girl is?* (She is the other girl's younger sister.) *What does she do?* (She takes the quilt.)

- **Pages 4–5** *Now what happens?* (The older sister doesn't want a book, so the younger one takes it.) *Do you think the younger sister is glad to have the book? How do you know?* (Yes. She says, "Oh, good!" which means she is glad to have the book.)

- **Pages 6–7** *What does the older sister get rid of now?* (a shirt) *Why do you think she is getting rid of this shirt?* (It looks like it is too small to fit her anymore.)

- **Page 7** *What do you think will happen next?* (The older sister will get rid of something else. The younger sister will take it and say, "Oh, good!")

- **Page 9** *Compare the picture of the younger sister on page 7 with this picture. What is different?* (The younger sister is now wearing the shirt her older sister didn't want.)

- **Pages 10–13** *What does the younger sister now have?* (a cup and a hat)

- **Pages 14–15** *What does the younger sister do with all the new things she has?* (She has made a house out of the blanket and some chairs. She is playing with all the new things.) *How do you think the younger sister feels? How do you think the older sister feels?* (The younger sister feels good because she has all the things, which are new to her. Maybe the older sister feels left out. Maybe she is asking if her sister will share with her.)

- **Page 16** *What do you think both sisters learned in this book?* (It seems that both sisters realize that it's more fun to share.)

Reading Strategies

If...	Then...
If... a child relies exclusively on the rebuses to read new words,	**Then...** have the child reread the book, using his or her letter-sound knowledge to decode the new words.
If... a child has trouble noticing the sentence patterns in the story,	**Then...** have him or her reread pages 2 and 4, and compare the words.
If... a child has difficulty drawing logical conclusions,	**Then...** use **Model Your Thinking** below.

Model Your Thinking

Think ALOUD

Comprehension Skill: Drawing Conclusions

As I read, I think about the characters and what happens in the story. I use word and picture clues, as well as what I already know from my own life, to figure out what the characters are like and what happens in the story. In this book, I see an older girl looking through her things and throwing out items that she doesn't want anymore. Each time she does this, a younger girl picks up the item and says, "Oh, good!" Her smile and her words tell me that she is happy to take the things. I know that in families, older brothers and sisters often give their younger brothers and sisters things they no longer want or have outgrown. That is what I think is happening here. As I keep reading, I will look to see what the younger sister will do with these items and how this makes the older sister feel.

After Reading

Revisiting the Text

Comprehension Have pairs read the book again. Children can use the T-Chart on page 140 to write words and/or draw pictures to show what each sister does in the story. Invite children to share their charts. Discuss each sister's actions and feelings.

9A
Jump Rope Time

by Kana Riley
Leveled Reader 9A
Genre: Realistic Story
Level: Easy

Summary

A girl's two friends, Jan and Tim, can jump rope. They are good at it, but she is not. She tries and tries, but just can't get the hang of it. After she tries some more, she makes a discovery. Now she can jump rope too!

Leveled Reader Practice

After children have read *Jump Rope Time,* use Leveled Reader practice page 157 to assess their understanding of the Leveled Reader and the target comprehension skill. Additional after reading activities are provided on page 43.

At a Glance

Links to the Student Edition

☞ **Comprehension Skill:** Main Idea

Selection Vocabulary: *jump, more, time*

Program Theme: Learning and Working
Unit Theme: Let's Learn Together

Trying and trying again, even when it seems hopeless, is one important way we learn.

Before Reading

Motivating the Reader
Build Background About Jumping Rope

Ask children if they know how to jump rope. Ask them if they think it is easy or difficult to jump rope well. Have them describe what it was like when they were first learning to jump rope. Encourage children to share how they felt and what finally happened. Invite volunteers to demonstrate how to jump rope. Ask children what they would say to someone who is having trouble learning to jump rope. Write their ideas on the chalkboard.

Preview and Predict

Have children scan the cover, text, and illustrations. Encourage them to use picture clues and familiar words to predict what the story is about. Prepare children for reading by saying:

> In this book, a girl wants to do something very much. Look through the book to see what it is she wants to do. Then read to see what happens. What do you think the story is about?

Point out selection vocabulary and other unfamiliar words that are important to understanding the book, such as *rope, but,* and *miss.*

During Reading

● Guiding Comprehension

Use the following questions to support children as they read.

- **Pages 2–3** *What do you think this book is about? What gives you that idea?* (The book must be about jumping rope. The title is "Jump Rope Time." Also these first two pages are all about jumping rope.)

- **Page 3** *Which girl is Jan? How do you know?* (Jan is the girl jumping rope. The words tell me that Jan is good at jumping rope.)

- **Page 5** *How are Jan and Tim alike?* (They are both good at jumping rope.)

- **Pages 6–7** *What is the girl's problem?* (She cannot jump rope. She keeps missing the jump.)

- **Pages 8–9** *What does the girl do? How do you think she feels?* (She keeps trying and trying. She looks sad and upset that she can't do it.)

- **Pages 10–11** *What happens to the girl? What do you think will happen next?* (She still misses. Maybe she will get better with practice.)

- **Page 11** *Do you think the girl should keep trying? Why or why not?* (Yes. The only way to learn how to do it right is to keep trying.)

- **Pages 12–13** *What happens now?* (She tries one more time and she doesn't miss. She is jumping rope.) *Why do you think she can now jump rope?* (Because she kept trying, she learned how to do it. Sometimes it just takes practice to learn to do something right.)

- **Pages 14–15** *How do you think the girl feels? How do you know?* (I think the girl is very happy. After trying and trying, she can finally jump rope with her friends. She looks very glad.)

- **Page 16** *What does all the time mean?* (It means "often" or "a lot.")

Reading Strategies

If...	Then...
If... a child stops at an unfamiliar word,	**Then...** ask him or her to read to the end of the sentence and predict what the word might be. Encourage the child to use knowledge about letters and sounds, as well as context clues, to figure out the word.
If... a child has difficulty reading *rope* and *time*,	**Then...** review the long *o* and the long *i* sounds (CVCe).
If... a child has difficulty identifying the book's main idea,	**Then...** use **Model Your Thinking** below.

Model Your Thinking

 Comprehension Skill: Main Idea

Think ALOUD

Every story tells about something. I look at the pictures and think about what happens in the story. I ask myself, "What is this book all about?" As I read, I see that each page is about jumping rope. Most of the pages are about a girl trying to jump rope like her friends can. Her friends are good jumpers. The girl is not. She tries and misses. She tries and misses again. She tries and tries—and suddenly it begins to happen. She can jump rope. The girl wanted to jump rope very much. She kept trying, and she learned how to do it!

After Reading

Revisiting the Text

Comprehension Invite children to reread the story and then retell it as a group. Make a large version of the Plot/Story Sequence organizer on page 134 and use it to write the outline. Ask children to tell what happens in the beginning, middle, and end. Write their ideas in the appropriate boxes. Finally, have them come up with one sentence that tells what the book is all about.

9B
Sleepy Pig

by Linda Lott
Leveled Reader 9B
Genre: Realistic Story
Level: Easy/Average

Summary

All the animals on the farm are working, but not Pig. Pig wants to sleep—until the one thing happens that gets Pig's attention. Bob and Dan pour out a bag of food. Now Pig wants to eat!

Leveled Reader Practice

After children have read *Sleepy Pig,* use Leveled Reader practice page 158 to assess their understanding of the Leveled Reader and the target comprehension skill. Additional after reading activities are provided on page 45.

At a Glance

Links to the Student Edition

☞ **Comprehension Skill:** Main Idea

Selection Vocabulary: *sleep, with*

Program Theme: Learning and Working
Unit Theme: Let's Learn Together

Everyone on the farm learns the importance of working together—except for a sleepy pig.

Before Reading

Motivating the Reader
Build Background About Farm Animals

Ask children to name some farm animals and tell about the characteristics of each animal. For example, cows moo and give milk, while hens cluck and lay eggs. Dogs like to run and chase. Horses carry people or pull loads. Then ask children what they think pigs do. Write children's ideas on the chalkboard. Encourage children to compare their ideas with the pig's actions as they read the book.

Preview and Predict

Have children scan the cover, text, and illustrations. Encourage them to use picture clues and familiar words to predict what the story is about. Prepare children for reading by saying:

> Each picture shows Pig. Can you find him? What do you learn about Pig by looking at the cover and the pictures? Is Pig like the other animals and people in the story? Read to find out what Pig wants to do.

Point out selection vocabulary and other unfamiliar words that are important to understanding the book, such as *works, help,* and *eat.*

During Reading

● Guiding Comprehension

Use the following questions to support children as they read.

- **Pages 2–3** **What characters do we find out about on these pages? What are they doing?** (We find out about Duck and Pig. Duck works, while Pig sleeps.)

- **Pages 4–5** **How does Hen work? What is Pig doing?** (Hen is collecting eggs. Pig just sleeps.)

- **Pages 6–7** **Now who is working? What work do they do?** (Dog and Puppy are chasing raccoons away from the corn.) **What is Pig doing?** (Pig is sleeping.)

- **Page 7** **What do you think will happen next?** (The book will show another animal working hard while Pig sleeps.)

- **Pages 8–9** **How does Cow work? What is Pig doing now?** (Cow gives milk. Pig is still sleeping.)

- **Page 9** **What words would you use to describe Pig?** (lazy, sleepy, not helpful)

- **Page 10** Point to the word *Horse*. **What is this word? Look at the picture and think about the word's beginning sound.** (horse)

- **Page 11** **How is Pig different from the other animals on the farm?** (They all work, but Pig likes to sleep.)

- **Pages 12–13** **Who is coming now? What work do you think they are doing? How can you tell?** (Bob and Dan are coming, carrying big sacks. Maybe there is food in the sacks. Pig is opening his eyes, and one ear is raised.)

- **Pages 14–15** **What makes Pig wake up?** (He sees food.) **What does Pig want?** (He wants to eat.)

- **Page 16** **How do you think Pig feels? How do you know?** (Pig is happy. He says, "Yum!" and has a smile on his face.)

Reading Strategies

If... a child hesitates at one or more of the animal names,	Then... have the child use his or her letter-sound knowledge to decode the words, and use the pictures and context clues to check the meaning.
If... a child hesitates at the change of pattern on page 6 or page 12,	Then... model fluent reading for him or her.
If... a child has difficulty identifying the book's main idea,	Then... use **Model Your Thinking** below.

Model Your Thinking

 Comprehension Skill: Main Idea

Think ALOUD

As I read, I ask myself, "What is this book all about?" I look at the pictures and think about what happens. On each page I see animals working while Pig sleeps. The only thing that makes Pig wake up is food. This book is about a sleeping pig who doesn't work, but who loves to eat!

After Reading

Revisiting the Text

Comprehension Have children reread the story. Have them write the book title in the center of Web 1 and write words and/or draw pictures to tell things that happen in the book. Have children use their webs to write a statement telling what the book is all about.

10A
Molly and Polly

by Sharon Fear
Leveled Reader 10A
Genre: Humorous Story
Level: Easy

Summary

Molly teaches Polly, her pet parrot, to speak. Later Molly and her dad hear someone speaking. They are puzzled, because only their dog is in the room with them. But they get a big surprise when they discover it was Polly who was speaking from the other room.

Leveled Reader Practice

After children have read *Molly and Polly,* use Leveled Reader practice page 159 to assess their understanding of the Leveled Reader and the target comprehension skill. Additional after reading activities are provided on page 47.

At a Glance

Links to the Student Edition

◎ **Comprehension Skill:** Classifying

Selection Vocabulary: *us, our*

Program Theme: Learning and Working
Unit Theme: Let's Learn Together

Learning new things can not only enrich our lives, but can also lead to big surprises.

Before Reading

Motivating the Reader
Build Background About Parrots

Show students pictures of real parrots and ask them to share what they know about these birds. Explain that parrots, and some other kinds of birds, can be taught to say words. You can train a parrot to talk by saying the same word over and over again until it learns to imitate the sound. Discuss how a talking parrot is different from a talking person.

Preview and Predict

Have children scan the cover, text, and illustrations. Encourage them to use picture clues and familiar words to predict what the story is about. Prepare children for reading by saying:

> *Where on the page are the words in this book?* (The words are in speech balloons at the tops of the pages.)
> *As you read the book, notice who is speaking. Read to find out which characters speak and which ones do not.*

Point out selection vocabulary and other unfamiliar words that are important to understanding the book, such as *say, yes, did, what, that,* and *tell.*

During Reading

Guiding Comprehension

Use the following questions to support children as they read.

- **Pages 2–3** *Who are the characters on these pages? What are they doing?* (Molly is ringing a bell and teaching her parrot, Polly, to say *bell*.)

- **Page 3** *What kind of bird is Polly?* (a parrot) *How do you know?* (Parrots have bright colors and can talk.)

- **Pages 4–5** *What word does Molly teach Polly next?* (Molly teaches Polly to say "cracker.") *How many times does Polly say "cracker"?* (Polly says it three times.)

- **Page 6** *Do you think Molly is glad that Polly learned to say "cracker"? How do you know?* (Yes, Molly is glad because she is giving Polly a cracker. Also, there are exclamation marks at the ends of the sentences. Molly is excited.)

- **Pages 8–9** *What other pets does Molly have?* (a cat and a dog) *What do Molly and her father think is happening?* (They think the dog is speaking to them.)

- **Page 10** *Why do you think Molly says, "Our dog cannot say that!"?* (She knows a dog cannot talk.)

- **Page 11** *Do you think the dog is talking? Why or why not?* (No, the dog is not talking. I think Polly is talking because the words said are the same words that Molly just taught Polly.)

- **Pages 12–13** *Who is Molly's father talking to?* (to the dog)

- **Pages 14–15** *Who is Molly speaking to?* (to Polly)

- **Page 16** *Was the dog speaking? How can you tell?* (No, Polly was speaking. She said the same words Molly taught her. She says "Yes, yes, yes!" which means she was the one talking.)

Reading Strategies

If...	Then...
If... a child seems disoriented by the speech balloons,	**Then...** have him or her track the words with a finger. Remind the child that we read from left to right.
If... a child hesitates, but then says the correct word,	**Then...** ask the child how he or she knew what the word was. This will help the child become aware of strategies he or she uses when reading.
If... a child has difficulty sorting and classifying information,	**Then...** use **Model Your Thinking** below.

Model Your Thinking

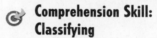 **Comprehension Skill: Classifying**

Think ALOUD

As I read this book, I noticed that Molly and her dad aren't sure who is talking. I can understand what is happening if I sort the characters into two groups: Characters Who Talk and Characters Who Don't Talk. Molly, Polly, and Molly's dad are all characters who talk. The cat is a character who doesn't talk. Once I read page 16, I find out for sure that it was Polly, not the dog, who was talking, so I put the dog in the same group as the cat.

After Reading

Revisiting the Text

Comprehension Have children reread the book and use the T-Chart on page 140 to keep track of who is speaking. At the top of the columns, write the heads *Can Talk* and *Cannot Talk*. Have children sort the characters into these two categories. Invite children to describe other ways to sort story information into groups, such as *People* and *Animals*.

10B

The Zookeeper

by Lisa Olsson
Leveled Reader 10B
Genre: Informational Article
Level: Easy/Average

Summary

A zookeeper brings different foods to a variety of hungry zoo animals. We see the animals in their natural habitats and learn about their favorite foods.

Leveled Reader Practice

After children have read *The Zookeeper*, use Leveled Reader practice page 160 to assess their understanding of the Leveled Reader and the target comprehension skill. Additional after reading activities are provided on page 49.

At a Glance

Links to the Student Edition

☞ **Comprehension Skill:** Classifying

Selection Vocabulary: *bring, carry, hold*

Program Theme: Learning and Working
Unit Theme: Let's Learn Together

We can learn a great deal by listening to others share their experiences. A zookeeper tells what her job is like.

Before Reading

Motivating the Reader
Build Background About Zoos

Ask children if they have visited a zoo, and have volunteers tell what it was like. If possible, show some pictures of real zoos. Explain that in some zoos, there are very few cages. Instead, the animals roam freely in large spaces that are like their natural habitats, the places where these animals live in the wild. Have children imagine they are zookeepers in charge of running the zoo and taking care of the animals. Use a web like Web 1 on page 131 to record children's ideas of what zookeepers do.

Preview and Predict

Have children scan the cover, text, and illustrations. Encourage them to use picture clues and familiar words to predict what the story is about. Prepare children for reading by saying:

> Imagine what it would be like to feed an elephant, a bear, or a zebra. How would you feel, being so close to a large animal? Let's read to find out what the zookeeper says about each animal.

Point out selection vocabulary and other unfamiliar words that are important to understanding the book, such as *more, hay, love,* and *job.*

During Reading

● Guiding Comprehension

Use the following questions to support children as they read.

- **Page 2** *Who do you think is speaking? How do you know?* (The person who feeds the animals is speaking. The title tells me she is a zookeeper.)

- **Page 3** *What does the zookeeper feed the elephant?* (The zookeeper feeds an apple to the elephant.) *Do you think one apple is enough for the elephant? Why or why not?* (No. An elephant is a very big animal, so one apple probably isn't enough. Also, the words say that the elephant wants more.)

- **Pages 4–5** *What does the zookeeper feed the bear? Do you think she will get as close as she did to the elephant? Why or why not?* (The zookeeper brings fish to the bear. I think she'll put the fish on the rocks and let the bear eat them. She won't get too close. Bears can be dangerous.)

- **Pages 6–7** *What does the giraffe eat?* (The giraffe eats leaves that the zookeeper is holding.) *How do you think giraffes' long necks help them eat?* (Their long necks help them eat leaves from tall trees.)

- **Pages 8–9** *Does the fox eat the carrots? How do you know?* (Yes. The words say that the fox eats the carrots.)

- **Pages 10–11** *What does the monkey eat?* (a banana) *Which food word shows one and which shows more than one?* (*Banana* shows one. *Bananas* shows more than one.)

- **Pages 12–13** *What does the zookeeper feed the zebras?* (She feeds them hay.)

- **Pages 14–15** *What does the zookeeper feed the fawn?* (a bottle of milk)

- **Page 16** *Why do you think the zookeeper loves her job?* (She gets to care for the animals every day.)

Reading Strategies

If... a child hesitates at the words *eats* and *wants* on page 7,	**Then...** cover the *s* and have the child read each base word. Then have him or her read it with the inflected ending.
If... a child points out that the sentence pattern changes on page 15,	**Then...** praise him or her for remembering what he or she has read.
If... a child has difficulty sorting and classifying information,	**Then...** use **Model Your Thinking** below.

Model Your Thinking

↻ **Comprehension Skill: Classifying**

Think ALOUD

As I read and learn about the animals, I can put them into groups. This will help me keep track of the different kinds of animals that are in the zoo. I can group the animals in many ways. For example, some of the animals are very big. The elephant, the giraffe, and the bear are large. I could put them in a group called Big Animals. But the monkey and the fox are small. They belong in a group called Small Animals. Putting these animals into groups helps me better understand how the animals are alike and different.

After Reading

Revisiting the Text

Comprehension Give pairs fourteen index cards. Have them reread the book and write all the foods mentioned on seven of the cards. Have them do the same for the animals. Have pairs mix the cards and exchange them. Children should sort the food and animal names cards into two columns. Have them align the rows so that each food card is next to the appropriate animal card.

11A
Wash Day

by Sydnie Meltzer Kleinhenz
Leveled Reader 11A
Genre: Realistic Story
Level: Easy

Summary

A boy brings out a tub, soap, and water and washes his bike. Seeing him, his sister, mother, and father each bring something to wash. They rub and rub—until they discover how dirty they have become! Then they all wash up too.

Leveled Reader Practice

After children have read *Wash Day,* use Leveled Reader practice page 161 to assess their understanding of the Leveled Reader and the target comprehension skill. Additional after reading activities are provided on page 51.

At a Glance

Links to the Student Edition

Comprehension Skill: Context Clues

Selection Vocabulary: *came, out, there, she*

Program Theme: Learning and Working
Unit Theme: Let's Learn Together

Working together makes the job easier and more fun.

Before Reading

Motivating the Reader
Build Background About Washing

Ask children the following questions to generate a discussion about washing.

> What have you helped wash? The car? The kitchen floor? Your dog? What materials did you use? Was it messy? What was the best part? What was the worst part?

Invite pairs or small groups of children to act out washing a bike, car, floor, or other household item.

Preview and Predict

Have children scan the cover, text, and illustrations. Encourage them to use picture clues and familiar words to predict what the story is about. Prepare children for reading by saying:

> There are several new words in this story. Use the story and the pictures to help you figure out the words. What do you think will happen on wash day? Read to find out.

Point out selection vocabulary and other unfamiliar words that are important to understanding the book, such as *got, her, looking, mess,* and *us.* Make sure children understand there are words in two places: in speech balloons at the top of the page and grouped in sentences at the bottom of the page.

During Reading

● Guiding Comprehension

Use the following questions to support children as they read.

- **Page 2** Point to the word *soap*. **What is this word? Look at the picture and think about what word makes sense here. Use the beginning and end sounds of the word to help you figure it out.** (soap) Repeat this type of questioning for other unfamiliar words.

- **Pages 2–3 What is the boy doing on these two pages? Why do you think he is doing this?** (The boy gets a bottle of soap and a tub. He must be getting ready to wash something.)

- **Pages 4–5 What is the boy washing?** (He is washing his bike.) **How do you think the boy feels? How can you tell?** (He feels good. He is smiling. He says his bike looks good.)

- **Pages 6–7 Who comes outside?** (Pam, the boy's sister) **What does she do?** (She brings her bike outside.) **Why do you think she does this?** (She wants to wash her bike too.)

- **Page 8 Do you remember seeing these words before? Where did you see them?** (Yes. The same words are on page 5.) **What is looking good?** (Pam's bike)

- **Page 9 Who comes out next?** (Mama comes out.) **What do you think will happen?** (She will wash something.)

- **Pages 10–11 What happens?** (Mama brings out chairs, and everyone washes them.)

- **Pages 12–13 Who comes out now?** (Papa comes out.) **What does he want to do?** (He wants to wash the car.)

- **Pages 14–15 What happens to the family as they wash? How do you know?** (They get dirty. They say, "What a mess!" The boy sees his dirty face in the car mirror.)

- **Page 16 What do these words mean? How do you know?** (The whole family is now looking good because they have washed. Their faces are clean. The children are wearing towels. Mama is drying Pam's hair.)

Reading Strategies

If... a child does not recognize the sentence patterns,	**Then...** reread the story with the child, running your finger under the words. Make the child aware of the rhythm to help make the words more memorable.
If... a child hesitates at new words,	**Then...** use **Model Your Thinking** below.

Model Your Thinking

 Comprehension Skill: Context Clues

Think
ALOUD

When good readers find a word they don't know, they look for clues in the pictures and think about what word makes sense in the sentence. They also look at the letters in the word and think about what sounds these letters stand for. For example, on page 2, I see the boy is holding a towel and a bottle of soap for washing dishes. I think about the beginning sounds and end sounds of the last word. I think this word is *soap.* I read the sentence: *I got the soap.* This word makes sense in the sentence. As I read and find other words I don't know, I will repeat these same steps to figure out what the word means.

After Reading

Revisiting the Text

Comprehension Make up sets of word cards by writing important story words on index cards. Give a set of cards to small groups. Have group members take turns reading the word on the card, finding it in the book, and using context clues to figure out its meaning. Have each group decide if the meaning is correct. Children can draw pictures or write definitions on the back of the cards.

11B

Looking for the Queen

by Gordon L. Storey
Leveled Reader 11B
Genre: Humorous Story
Level: Easy/Average

Summary

Everyone in the palace is looking for the queen. But the queen is having fun, floating in the pool on a raft. When everyone sees how happy she is and how much fun she is having, they grab rafts and tubes and join her in the pool!

Leveled Reader Practice

After children have read *Looking for the Queen,* use Leveled Reader practice page 162 to assess their understanding of the Leveled Reader and the target comprehension skill. Additional after reading activities are provided on page 53.

At a Glance

Links to the Student Edition

☞ **Comprehension Skill:** Context Clues

Selection Vocabulary: *know, she, there*

Program Theme: Learning and Working
Unit Theme: Let's Learn Together

Working together is important, but learning to relax and have fun is important too.

Before Reading

Motivating the Reader
Build Background About Queens

Ask children to talk about queens in folk tales:

> What *does* a queen usually wear?
>
> What *does* a queen do?
>
> Describe a good queen and a bad queen.

Invite children to draw pictures of what they think a queen in a story might look like. Have them share their finished drawings and ideas about queens.

Preview and Predict

Have children scan the cover, text, and illustrations. Draw their attention to the characters on each page to help them see that as the story progresses the number of people looking for the queen grows. Encourage them to use picture clues and familiar words to predict what the story is about. Prepare children for reading by saying:

> We're going to read a story about a missing queen. Who do you think is looking for the queen? Why do they want to find her? Read to find out where the queen is and what she is doing.

Point out selection vocabulary and other unfamiliar words that are important to understanding the book, such as *having, fun, here,* and *well.*

During Reading

Guiding Comprehension

Use the following questions to support children as they read.

- **Page 2** Point to the word *know*. **What is this word? Think about the other words in the sentence. What word makes sense here?** (know) Encourage children to use context clues to figure out the meanings of other unfamiliar words.

- **Page 2 Why is the man looking for the queen?** (There are jobs for her to do.)

- **Page 3 How is this palace different from other ones you have read about?** (It has phones, computers, and telephone poles.)

- **Page 4 Why is the woman looking for the queen? How do you know?** (There are phone calls for her. The words say there are calls for the queen. The woman is holding telephones.)

- **Page 6 Why is this woman looking for the queen?** (There are letters for her to read and sign.)

- **Page 7 Do you see any patterns in the words so far?** (Children should clearly articulate the sentence patterns of the first six pages.)

- **Pages 8–9 Who is asking for help from the queen?** (A cook with an apron and a pan, and a knight in armor with a sword.)

- **Page 9 Why are there three points on this speech balloon?** (All three characters are saying these words together.)

- **Pages 10–11 Where do they find the queen?** (They find her outside the palace.)

- **Page 14 What is the queen doing?** (She is having fun floating in a swimming pool.)

- **Page 15 What do you think the people mean when they say, "Well, she is the queen!"?** (They mean that a queen can do anything she wants.)

- **Page 16 What do the people do?** (They join the queen in the swimming pool.)

Ongoing Assessment

Reading Strategies

If... a child has trouble telling who is speaking,	**Then...** help the child trace a path from the point of the speech balloon to the speaking character. Point out places where people speak as a group.
If... a child calls attention to the repeated use of certain words,	**Then...** praise him or her for paying attention to sentence patterns.
If... a child has difficulty using context clues to figure out unknown words,	**Then...** use **Model Your Thinking** below.

Model Your Thinking

 Comprehension Skill: Context Clues

Think ALOUD

When good readers find a word they don't know, they look for clues in the pictures nearby and think about what the sentence means. They also look at the letters in the word they don't know and think about what sounds the letters stand for. For example, on page 6, there is one word repeated four times. I see that the woman speaking is holding pieces of paper and a pen. Earlier, on page 5, this same woman was writing on these pages. The first three letters of this word spell a word I know—*let*. I see an *s* on the end of the word. I think this word is *letters*. I reread the sentences to see if *letters* makes sense. It does, so I know the woman has letters for the queen.

After Reading

Revisiting the Text

Comprehension Have children use the T-Chart on page 140. Have them review the book and list words they didn't know on the left side of their charts. On the right side they can write words or draw pictures to show what each word means.

12A

Do What I Do

by Nat Gabriel
Leveled Reader 12A
Genre: Humorous Story
Level: Easy

Summary

A young girl teaches a pig to dance by demonstrating the dance steps. At first the pig is clumsy, and the pair fall into the mud. After some more practice, they dance happily around the pig pen. Finally the girl decides to do what the pig does—take a nap.

Leveled Reader Practice

After children have read *Do What I Do,* use Leveled Reader practice page 163 to assess their understanding of the Leveled Reader and the target comprehension skill. Additional after reading activities are provided on page 55.

At a Glance

Links to the Student Edition

↻ **Comprehension Skill:** Character

Selection Vocabulary: *read, say, word*

Program Theme: Learning and Working
Unit Theme: Let's Learn Together

It's always important to be patient when you're working with others. It takes a lot of practice to learn to do something new.

Before Reading

Motivating the Reader
Build Background About Teaching

Ask children to tell about a time when someone helped them learn something, such as tying their shoes or riding a bike. Have them describe how the person taught them what to do. Ask them whether it was easy or hard for them to learn. Discuss the characteristics of a good teacher, such as someone who is patient, shows you how to do things, and gives clear directions that are easy to follow. Invite volunteers to teach the class something simple, such as how to dance or how to cut out a paper shape.

Preview and Predict

Have children scan the cover, text, and illustrations. Encourage them to use picture clues and familiar words to predict what the story is about. Prepare children for reading by saying:

> In this story, a girl tries to teach something. What does she teach? Who is her student? You can learn about a character through what he or she does and says. Read to find out what the girl and the pig are like.

Point out the selection vocabulary and other unfamiliar words that are important to understanding the book, such as *dance, left* (directional), *step,* and *nap.*

During Reading

Guiding Comprehension

Use the following questions to support children as they read.

- **Pages 2–3** *Who is speaking?* (The girl is talking to the pig.) *What does she want to do?* (She wants to teach the pig how to dance.)

- **Pages 4–5** *How does the girl teach the pig to dance? How can you tell?* (She shows the pig what steps to make. In the picture, the pig is looking at her while she dances. Also she tells the pig to do what she does.)

- **Pages 6–7** *What happens now?* (The pig steps on the girl's foot.)

- **Page 8** *How does the girl behave after the pig steps on her foot?* (She does the steps for the pig again. She isn't mad or upset that he made a mistake.)

- **Page 9** *What happens here?* (The pig falls on the girl.)

- **Page 9** *What will happen next?* (The girl will show the pig the steps again.)

- **Pages 12–13** *Do you think the pig is learning? How do you know?* (The pig is doing much better. Both the girl and the pig have smiles on their faces. Also the girl says "There we go!" which means they are dancing.)

- **Pages 14–15** *Is the pig getting any better at dancing?* (Yes. The girl tells the pig that he is good at dancing. Also, in the pictures, the girl and the pig are twirling and smiling.)

- **Page 16** *How do the girl and the pig feel after dancing?* (They are happy because the pig learned to dance. But they must be tired because they both take naps.)

- **Page 16** *What words would you use to tell what the girl is like?* (patient, nice, smart, graceful, calm) *What words would you use to tell what the pig is like?* (clumsy at first, but then graceful; tries hard; patient)

Ongoing Assessment

Reading Strategies

If... a child hesitates but then says the correct word,	**Then...** ask the child how he or she knew what the word was.
If... a child reads *left* correctly,	**Then...** praise the child for paying close attention to ending sounds.
If... a child has difficulty drawing conclusions about characters,	**Then...** use **Model Your Thinking** below.

Model Your Thinking

Comprehension Skill: Character

Think ALOUD

A character is a person or animal in a story. You can figure out what characters are like and how they feel by thinking about what they say and do. In this book, a girl wants to teach a pig how to dance. She shows the pig some dance steps and says, "Do what I do." The pig stumbles and steps on her foot. I can see that it hurts, but she goes right on trying. This tells me that she is patient. She smiles at the pig. She looks upset when the pig falls, but she goes right on teaching him how to dance. She doesn't get mad or yell at him. The girl is a good dancer, and she has worked hard to teach the pig. I can see in the pictures on pages 14–15 that she is very happy that her lesson was a success.

After Reading

Revisiting the Text

Comprehension Draw a large version of Web 1 from page 131 and write *The Girl* in the center. Ask children to tell things they know about her from the story, and record these details around the outer spokes. Then have children make statements about the girl based on information from the web. Repeat for the pig.

12B

Peas Please

by Susan Hood
Leveled Reader 12B
Genre: Humorous Story
Level: Easy/Average

Summary

A young boy is trying to feed his baby sister. But she refuses to eat anything he offers her. As he's reaching over to her highchair for one last try, he falls out of his chair. The little girl laughs and finally asks for some peas.

Leveled Reader Practice

After children have read *Peas Please*, use Leveled Reader practice page 164 to assess their understanding of the Leveled Reader and the target comprehension skill. Additional after reading activities are provided on page 57.

At a Glance

Links to the Student Edition

☞ **Comprehension Skill:** Character

Selection Vocabulary: *please, again*

Program Theme: Learning and Working
Unit Theme: Let's Learn Together

Sometimes we learn that success can come from unfortunate events.

Before Reading

Motivating the Reader
Build Background About Feeding a Baby

Ask children if they have ever fed a baby. Ask them to describe the experience. Discuss the kinds of foods babies eat and the typical behaviors babies display when being fed. Invite volunteers to share any tips they have for getting picky eaters to eat, such as making airplane sounds and movements. Then have children draw pictures of an older sibling feeding a baby.

Preview and Predict

Have children scan the cover, text, and illustrations. Encourage them to use picture clues and familiar words to predict what the story is about. Prepare children for reading by saying:

> Do you think feeding the little girl is easy for this boy? How do you think he feels? Read to find out about the boy and the girl. What are they like?

Point out selection vocabulary and other unfamiliar words that are important to understanding the book, such as *peas, plums, carrots,* and *corn.*

During Reading

Guiding Comprehension

Use the following questions to support children as they read.

- **Pages 2–3** *What is the boy doing?* (He is trying to get his sister to eat some peas.)

- **Page 4** *Does his sister want the peas? How do you know?* (No, she does not. She shakes her head and says, "No! No peas!")

- **Page 4** *Look at these marks after these words. What do you think the little sister sounds like when she says these words?* (She sounds upset.) Encourage children to read the words aloud with proper intonation.

- **Page 5** *What is the boy trying to feed the girl now?* (He is trying to feed her plums.)

- **Page 6** *What does the girl do now?* (She tries to cover her face with her bib so that she doesn't have to eat the plums. She says, "No! No plums!")

- **Page 7** *What is the boy like? How do you know?* (He is patient since he keeps trying to feed his sister even though she keeps saying no. He is nice since he doesn't get mad and keeps saying please.)

- **Page 8** *What is the baby sister like? How do you know?* (She is very stubborn and a fussy eater. She says no to all the foods her brother offers her. She covers her face with her bib so he can't feed her.)

- **Page 11** *How do you think the boy feels now?* (He is frustrated. He has a sad look on his face. He says these words as a question.)

- **Pages 12–13** *How is the baby behaving? How does the boy feel?* (The baby sticks out her tongue and plays with her toy. The boy feels hopeless. You can tell by the way he sits and by the look on his face.)

- **Page 16** *What has happened? Who says these words?* (The boy has fallen out of his chair, and his baby sister thinks it is funny. The baby sister says these words. Now she wants to eat some peas!)

Reading Strategies

If... a child reads without proper intonation,	**Then...** call attention to the commas and exclamation points and discuss their meanings.
If... a child loses track of the number of *no's* or *please's*,	**Then...** suggest that the child read with a finger to track the words.
If... a child has difficulty drawing conclusions about characters,	**Then...** use **Model Your Thinking** below.

Model Your Thinking

 Comprehension Skill: Character

 Think ALOUD

Characters are the people or animals in a story. In this book, the characters act like children I know. The brother and his baby sister both have strong feelings. I can tell how they feel by what they say and by how they look. The boy really wants his sister to eat the peas. He says, "Please! Please!" The little girl doesn't feel like eating. First she shakes her head and says "No!" Then she covers her mouth with a bib, and then with her hands. She knocks the spoon of corn away. She is stubborn. She really *does not want to eat!* The brother is patient and nice. He does not get mad when she won't eat, and he keeps saying please. By the end of the story, he probably thinks she will never eat. She finally is willing to eat after he falls off his chair!

After Reading

Revisiting the Text

Comprehension Have children reread the book and draw a picture to show their favorite part of the story. Invite children to describe their pictures, explaining who the characters are, what they are doing, and how they feel.

13A
Jump, Jump

by Anne Phillips
Leveled Reader 13A
Genre: Song
Level: Easy

Summary

This lively jump-rope song ropes in the whole family, all moving as fast as they can, until Baby joins in. Oops! They all fall down.

Leveled Reader Practice

After children have read *Jump, Jump,* use Leveled Reader practice page 165 to assess their understanding of the Leveled Reader and the target comprehension skill. Additional after reading activities are provided on page 59.

At a Glance

Links to the Student Edition

↻ **Comprehension Skill:** Realism and Fantasy

Selection Vocabulary: *call, as*

Program Theme: Traditions
Unit Theme: Favorite Things Old and New

Everyone has a favorite traditional pastime, such as jumping rope. These pastimes are more fun when you can share them with others.

Before Reading

Motivating the Reader
Build Background About Jumping Rope

Provide a big jump rope (or have children pantomime, using an imaginary rope). Have two children turn the rope slowly. Other children should line up and then jump through the rope once and go back to the beginning. Then have three people jump together, jumping in one at a time, to a total of six jumps. Have children turn the rope and jump until everyone has had a chance to jump. Then ask:

> What's easy about jumping rope? What is hard? Could more than three people jump together? How many more?

Preview and Predict

Have children scan the cover, text, and illustrations. Encourage them to use picture clues and familiar words to predict what the story is about. Prepare children for reading by saying:

> Look at the pictures and words. What are these people doing? Who do you think these people are? Let's read to find out what happens as more and more people try to jump rope at the same time.

Point out the selection vocabulary and other unfamiliar words that are important to understanding the book, such as the names for different family members.

During Reading

Guiding Comprehension

Use the following questions to support children as they read.

- **Page 2** What is the little girl doing on this page? (She is jumping rope.) **Which word tells you how she jumps?** (fast)

- **Page 3** What does it mean to "call in" someone when you are jumping rope? (It means to call or yell for someone to jump in and begin jumping rope.) **Who is called in to start jumping?** (Father is called in to start jumping.)

- **Pages 4–5** How many people are jumping rope? (Two people are jumping.) **Do you think this could really happen?** (Yes. Two people can jump rope at the same time.)

- **Pages 6–7** Who is called in now? (Mother is called in.)

- **Page 8** How many people are jumping now? (Three people are jumping.)

- **Page 8** What do you think will happen next? (Another member of the family will be called in to jump with those already jumping rope.)

- **Page 9** Now who is called in? (Sister is called in.)

- **Pages 10–11** How many people are jumping rope now? (Four people are jumping rope.) **Do you think it is easier or more difficult to jump with a lot of people? Why?** (It gets more difficult as more people jump because someone will probably make a mistake and miss.)

- **Page 14** How many people are jumping rope now? (Five people are jumping.)

- **Page 15** What do you think will happen when Baby is called in? (I think Baby won't be able to jump rope. Also, there are so many people jumping rope that I think the rope will get tangled.)

- **Page 16** What happened? (The family fell down.)

Reading Strategies

If.... a child picks up the sentence pattern, but starts reading too quickly and skips words,

Then... help him or her slow down by visually tracking text with a finger.

If.... a child has trouble distinguishing events that could really happen and events that could not really happen,

Then... use **Model Your Thinking** below.

Model Your Thinking

Comprehension Skill: Realism and Fantasy

Think ALOUD

Some stories tell about things that could really happen. Other stories are make-believe. They include things that could not really happen. As I read about something a character does in the story, I ask myself: "Could this really happen?" In this book, a family is jumping rope together. First, one girl jumps. Then her father jumps with her. Now there are two people jumping. Pretty soon there are five people jumping. When Baby tries to jump, then everyone gets tangled up in the rope and falls down. I know these events could really happen because I've seen people jump rope together. I know that the more people who jump, the more likely it is that someone will miss. Since this book tells about things that could really happen, I know this book isn't make-believe.

After Reading

Revisiting the Text

Comprehension Take a vote on whether children think this book tells about things that could really happen or if it is make-believe. Encourage children to give reasons for their votes. Then have volunteers act out the story while other children do a choral reading.

13B
Biff Helps After All

by Nat Gabriel
Leveled Reader 13B
Genre: Humorous Story
Level: Easy/Average

Summary

A boy decorates his bike for a Fourth of July event with the help of his parents. When his dog, Biff, twists crepe paper around the bike, the boy thinks Biff has made a mess. But when the bike wins first prize, the boy decides that Biff helped after all.

Leveled Reader Practice

After children have read *Biff Helps After All,* use Leveled Reader practice page 166 to assess their understanding of the Leveled Reader and the target comprehension skill. Additional after reading activities are provided on page 61.

At a Glance

Links to the Student Edition

Comprehension Skill: Realism and Fantasy

Selection Vocabulary: *after, catch, something, laugh*

Program Theme: Traditions
Unit Theme: Favorite Things Old and New

One way to celebrate the Fourth of July is to decorate with red, white, and blue. When a pet decides to help, unexpected things happen.

Before Reading

Motivating the Reader
Build Background About the Fourth of July

Ask children to discuss what they know about the Fourth of July. Ask what symbols, events, and foods are associated with the holiday. Invite children to talk about July Fourth celebrations they have enjoyed. Have pairs work together to draw a picture showing a traditional way people celebrate this holiday, such as a parade, a picnic, or fireworks.

Preview and Predict

Have children scan the cover, text, and illustrations. Encourage them to use picture clues and familiar words to predict what the story is about. Prepare children for reading by saying:

> Who do you think is telling this story? Who is Biff? What is happening in the story? As you read the book, pay attention to what the people and the dog do. Think about whether they are being helpful or not.

Point out the selection vocabulary and other unfamiliar words that are important to understanding the book, such as *today, day, a lot,* and *need.*

During Reading

Guiding Comprehension

Use the following questions to support children as they read.

- **Page 2** *What day do you think it is? How can you tell?* (It is the Fourth of July. It's circled on the calendar.)

- **Pages 2–3** *Who is telling this story?* (the boy) *Who is the boy talking to?* (the dog) *What is the dog's name?* (Biff)

- **Pages 4–5** *What is the boy doing?* (He is putting red crepe paper on his bike.)

- **Pages 6–7** *What is the boy doing now?* (He is putting white crepe paper on the bike.) *How do you think the boy feels? How do you know?* (The boy looks pleased. He says that the bike looks good.)

- **Page 8** *What is the boy doing now?* (The boy is decorating the bike wheel with blue crepe paper.)

- **Pages 10–11** *Who helps the boy?* (The boy's mother and father help him decorate the bike. His father puts a flag on the bike. His mother cuts out stars to put on the bike.)

- **Pages 12–13** *What happens now?* (Biff runs around with colored streamers. The family is trying to catch him. Biff is pulling streamers around the bike.)

- **Pages 14–15** *How do you think the boy feels? How can you tell?* (The boy is mad because Biff ruined his decorations. The boy is frowning. He said earlier that Biff wasn't helping.)

- **Page 16** *How do you think the boy feels at the end? Why?* (He is happy and proud. The bike looks good, and he won first prize. Also, he says, "Now we can laugh.")

- **Page 16** *Does this book tell about things that could really happen or is it a make-believe story? How do you know?* (It tells about things that could really happen. You can really decorate a bike, and a dog could play with the ribbons the way Biff does.)

Reading Strategies

If... a child misreads a word and stops,	**Then...** ask him or her to read to the end of the sentence and think about what word makes sense in the sentence.
If... a child has trouble distinguishing events that could really happen and events that could not really happen,	**Then...** use **Model Your Thinking** below.

Model Your Thinking

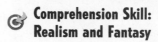 **Comprehension Skill: Realism and Fantasy**

 Think ALOUD

Some stories tell about things that really happen. Other stories are make-believe. They tell about things that could not really happen, such as animals talking. As I read about what happens in this book, I ask myself: "Could this really happen?" In this book, a boy decorates his bike with red, white, and blue ribbons. His mom and dad help him put flags and stars on his bike. His dog Biff runs around the bike and gets the ribbons wrapped all around the bike. These are all things that could really happen. I know people decorate with red, white, and blue on the Fourth of July. I also know parents often help their children, and pets can sometimes make a mess of things. I'm surprised when the boy's bike wins a prize, but I think it could happen. This story tells about things that could really happen.

After Reading

Revisiting the Text

Comprehension Have children reread the book and tell what happens. Use the Plot/Story Sequence organizer on page 134 to record each event as children tell it. Discuss whether these events could really happen.

14A
Mother's Day

by Fay Robinson
Leveled Reader 14A
Genre: Animal Fantasy
Level: Easy

Summary

On Mother's Day, Kitty made orange juice, cereal, tea, toast, and a pancake for her mother. She made a big mess too. After enjoying the breakfast, Kitty's mother got a big surprise when she saw the kitchen!

Leveled Reader Practice

After children have read *Mother's Day,* use Leveled Reader practice page 167 to assess their understanding of the Leveled Reader and the target comprehension skill. Additional after reading activities are provided on page 63.

At a Glance

Links to the Student Edition

🌀 **Comprehension Skill:** Theme

Selection Vocabulary: *every, of, made, was*

Program Theme: Traditions
Unit Theme: Favorite Things Old and New

Mother's Day is just one traditional holiday that lets us show a special person how much we love her.

Before Reading

Motivating the Reader
Build Background About Mother's Day

Ask children to name special celebrations that are given for a special person, such as birthdays or graduations. Ask children how they have participated in the celebrations. Then bring up Mother's Day and ask how children, their friends at school, and their families have celebrated Mother's Day. Record children's ideas in a large word web drawn on the chalkboard.

Preview and Predict

Have children scan the cover, text, and illustrations. Encourage them to use picture clues and familiar words to predict what the story is about. Prepare children for reading by saying:

> What is this story all about? How do you know? Read to find out what Kitty is doing and how she feels.

Point out the selection vocabulary and other unfamiliar words that are important to understanding the book, such as *love, singing, ate,* and *pleased.*

During Reading

● Guiding Comprehension

Use the following questions to support children as they read.

- **Pages 2–3 What special day was it? How do you know?** (It was Mother's Day. The words say it was Mother's Day and so does the sign on the wall.)

- **Pages 4–5 What did Kitty make?** (She made orange juice.) **Whom do you think she made it for? How do you know?** (She made it for her mother. She says, "Mom will love this!")

- **Pages 6–7 How do you think Kitty felt? How can you tell?** (I think she was happy. She is smiling, and it says that she was singing.)

- **Pages 8–9 Which word shows what Kitty made?** (toast) **Find the toast in the picture.** (Children should point out the toast.)

- **Page 10 Which word tells you how Kitty feels?** (pleased) **What is another word that means almost the same as pleased?** (glad, happy)

- **Pages 10–11 What words could you use to describe Kitty?** (Possible answers: caring, sweet, funny, messy)

- **Page 12** Point to *pancake*. **What is this word? What two smaller words are in this word?** (pancake; pan and cake)

- **Pages 14–15 Did Kitty's mother like what Kitty had done? How do you know?** (Yes. The words say that she was happy and pleased. She ate everything Kitty made.)

- **Page 16 How do you think Kitty's mother felt when she saw the kitchen?** (Possible answers: She was surprised. I don't think she was mad, but I don't think she expected to see such a mess. She was pleased because Kitty had done such a nice thing for her.)

- **Page 16 What is the big idea in this book?** (Possible answers: It's nice to do things for other people. Mothers like gifts made with love. Mother's Day is a day to show your mother how you feel about her.)

Reading Strategies

If... a child relies heavily on pictures to figure out new food words,	**Then...** encourage the child to look at the letters that represent the sounds.
If... a child hesitates at the word *pleased*,	**Then...** cover the *d* and encourage the child to decode the base word.
If... a child has trouble identifying the theme,	**Then...** use **Model Your Thinking** below.

Model Your Thinking

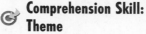

🎯 **Comprehension Skill: Theme**

 Think ALOUD

Most stories have a big idea. A big idea might be a lesson that a character learns. It might also be something the reader learns about people or life. To help me figure out what the big idea of this book is, I think about what happens in the story and what I know from my own life. In this book, Kitty makes a special breakfast for her mom for Mother's Day. Making the food for her mom makes Kitty happy. Kitty's breakfast makes Mom happy too. I know that it makes me happy to do something nice for someone. I also feel happy when someone does something nice for me. Even though Kitty made a mess of the kitchen, I think her mom will still like her surprise since Kitty worked so hard. A big idea of this story is: Doing something nice for someone can make that person happy. It can make you happy too.

After Reading

Revisiting the Text

Comprehension Invite children to tell in their own words what the book's big idea is. Assure children that there may be more than one big idea. Have children draw a picture that shows this big idea. Help children write captions for their pictures.

14B

Where Bat Came From

A Creek Tale

retold by Sharon Fear
Leveled Reader 14B
Genre: Folk Tale
Level: Easy/Average

Summary

Mouse is sad. All his friends can kick, run, and catch when playing ball. Mouse cannot. His mother encourages Mouse to practice by jumping. One day he jumps up, and he can fly. Now Mouse is Bat. And Bat can play ball!

Leveled Reader Practice

After children have read *Where Bat Came From,* use Leveled Reader practice page 168 to assess their understanding of the Leveled Reader and the target comprehension skill. Additional after reading activities are provided on page 65.

At a Glance

Links to the Student Edition

⌖ **Comprehension Skill:** Theme

Selection Vocabulary: *mother, every*

Program Theme: Traditions
Unit Theme: Favorite Things Old and New

Folk tales represent an important part of traditional literature—a culture's favorite stories passed down from generation to generation.

Before Reading

Motivating the Reader
Build Background About Playing Ball

Take children to a space where they can throw, catch, and kick balls, or plan to roll and toss balls in the classroom. Provide one or several soccer-size balls. Then have children talk about the feelings they might have if they were too small to play ball with their friends.

Preview and Predict

Have children scan the cover, text, and illustrations. Encourage them to use picture clues and familiar words to predict what the story is about. Prepare children for reading by saying:

> Who are the animals in this story? What problem do you think Mouse has? Let's read to find out how Mouse solves his problem.

Point out the selection vocabulary and other unfamiliar words that are important to understanding the book, such as *mouse, friend, plays, sad, fly,* and *bat.*

During Reading

Guiding Comprehension

Use the following questions to support children as they read.

- **Pages 2–3** **What is happening here?** (Mouse and his friends are playing ball.) **How is mouse different from his friends?** (His friends are much bigger than Mouse.)

- **Pages 4–5** **What can Mouse's friends do?** (They can kick the ball.) **Can Mouse do it too?** (No. He cannot kick the ball.) **Why can't Mouse kick the Ball?** (He is too small.)

- **Pages 6–7** **What else can Mouse's friends do?** (They can run.) **Can Mouse do what his friends can do?** (No. Mouse cannot run.)

- **Pages 8–9** **Which action word shows what Mouse's friends can do?** (catch) **What happens when Raccoon throws the ball?** (Mouse cannot catch it.) **Why does this happen?** (Mouse is too small to catch a ball this big.)

- **Page 10** **How does Mouse feel?** (Mouse is sad.) **Why do you think he feels this way?** (He is sad because he cannot play ball the way his friends can.)

- **Pages 11–13** **What does Mother Mouse tell Mouse to do?** (She tells him to jump over and over as she holds the ball above him.)

- **Page 12** Point to *again*. **What is this word?** (again) **What does Mother Mouse want Mouse to do?** (She wants him to jump one more time.)

- **Pages 14–15** **What happens to Mouse?** (One day he jumps up and can fly. Mouse turns into Bat.) **How does Mouse feel now?** (He is happy.)

- **Page 16** **How is Bat different from Mouse?** (Bat has wings. He can fly and play ball.)

- **Page 16** **What is the big idea of this book?** (Possible answers: If you try hard enough, you can sometimes do something you couldn't do before. Don't quit. It feels good to be able to do something well.)

Ongoing Assessment

Reading Strategies

If... a child is confused when Mouse turns into Bat,	**Then...** remind the child that some stories are make-believe and tell about things that couldn't really happen.
If... a child hesitates at the action words such as *kick, run, throw,* and *jump,*	**Then...** encourage the child to use letter-sound knowledge and picture clues to solve the word.
If... a child has trouble identifying the book's theme,	**Then...** use **Model Your Thinking** below.

Model Your Thinking

Comprehension Skill: Theme

Think ALOUD

Most stories have a big idea. The big idea can be a lesson a character learns. It can also be something a reader learns about people or life. To help me figure out this book's big idea, I think about what happens and what I know from my own life. In this book, Mouse wants to play ball with his friends. But he cannot do the things they can do, such as kick, run, and throw the ball. The ball is too big, and Mouse is too small. Then Mother Mouse tells Mouse to jump. He jumps and jumps. He tries very hard. And something wonderful happens. Mouse becomes Bat! Now he can play ball with his friends. I think the big idea is the importance of not giving up. If you keep trying, you may be able to do something you couldn't do before. I know that it sometimes takes a lot of practice to do something well.

After Reading

Revisiting the Text

Comprehension Have pairs reread the book and discuss its big idea. Students can use Web 1 on page 131 to record the theme in the center and reasons that support their answer around the outside. Have pairs share their webs.

15A
A Day for Dad

by Susan McCloskey
Leveled Reader 15A
Genre: Photo Essay
Level: Easy

Summary

It is Father's Day, so Ben lets his dad sleep late. He makes a card and a clay cat paperweight for his dad. He washes the car and helps his mom make pancakes for his dad. Then he wakes up his dad and gives him another gift— a big hug!

Leveled Reader Practice

After children have read *A Day for Dad,* use Leveled Reader practice page 169 to assess their understanding of the Leveled Reader and the target comprehension skill. Additional after reading activities are provided on page 67.

At a Glance

Links to the Student Edition

✪ **Comprehension Skill:** Main Idea

Selection Vocabulary: *father, very*

Program Theme: Traditions
Unit Theme: Favorite Things Old and New

Celebrating Father's Day is a great way to keep traditions alive and do something nice for a favorite family member.

Before Reading

Motivating the Reader
Build Background About Father's Day

Tell children that they will read a story about Father's Day. Ask them what they know about traditions that families have for celebrating Father's Day. Have them discuss what they think a father would like on his special day. Record children's responses on the chalkboard. If time permits have children act out one or two of the suggested ideas.

Preview and Predict

Have children scan the cover, text, and photographs. Encourage them to use picture clues and familiar words to predict what the story is about. Prepare children for reading by saying:

> **What do you think this book is all about? How do you know? As you read, pay attention to what Ben does to make the day special for his dad.**

Point out the selection vocabulary and other unfamiliar words that are important to understanding the book, such as *late, why, letting, making, wake,* and *gifts.*

During Reading

● Guiding Comprehension

Use the following questions to support children as they read.

- **Page 2** *Who is Ben?* (the boy in the photograph) *Who is in the bed?* (Ben's father)

- **Page 3** *What does shhh mean?* (It is a sound that means "be quiet.")

- **Page 3** *What is Ben letting his father do?* (Ben is letting his father sleep late.) *Why do you think Ben is doing this? How do you know?* (Possible answer: He's letting him sleep late because it is Father's Day or his birthday. The book is called "A Day for Dad.")

- **Page 4** *Why is Ben pointing at the calendar?* (He is showing what day it is— Father's Day.)

- **Page 5** *What does the heart mean on the card Ben is making?* (It means "love.")

- **Page 6** *Look at Ben. What is he doing?* (He is trying to think of what else he can do for his dad.)

- **Pages 8–9** *What is Ben doing?* (He is making a cat out of clay.) *What will Ben's father do with it?* (He will put it on his desk.)

- **Page 11** *What does Ben decide to do now?* (He washes his father's car with the help of his mother.)

- **Pages 12–13** *Why do you think Ben is doing all of these things for his father?* (Ben wants to do special things for his father on Father's Day. He is doing things that his father will like.)

- **Page 15** *What do you think Ben's last gift will be?* (Answers will vary.)

- **Page 16** *Why do you think Dad likes the hug best of all?* (Dad likes the hug because it shows that Ben loves him.)

- **Page 16** *What is this book all about?* (It is all about the nice things a son does for his dad on Father's Day.)

Reading Strategies

If... a child hesitates at the words *letting* or *making*,	Then... help the child relate the words to the more familiar base words, *let* and *make*. Then he or she can read the phrase, *is letting* or *is making* and go on to finish the page.
If... a child is uncertain of the words *card, cat, car,* and *gifts*,	Then... suggest that he or she read the rest of the sentence and look for word and picture clues that will help identify the words.
If... a child has difficulty identifying the book's main idea,	Then... use **Model Your Thinking** below.

Model Your Thinking

Think ALOUD

↻ Comprehension Skill: Main Idea

Every story is about something. You can tell what a story is about using your own words. This book tells all about the nice things Ben does for his dad on Father's Day. I see that Ben makes a card for his dad, but that is just a small part of the story. It doesn't tell what the whole story is about.

After Reading

Revisiting the Text

Comprehension List three choices about the book's main idea. Have pairs reread the book and pick the choice they think tells what the book is all about. Children can write the main idea in the Main Idea organizer on page 135. They can draw pictures in the boxes below to show smaller parts of the story.

15B
Karate Class

by Phoebe Marsh
Leveled Reader 15B
Genre: Informational Article
Level: Easy/Average

Summary

Readers follow the actions of a young girl in her karate class. Linn puts on her karate outfit and bows to her teacher. She yells a karate yell, and she kicks, blocks, and chops. Then, at the end of the class, Linn and the students bow a "Thank you" to the teacher.

Leveled Reader Practice

After children have read *Karate Class,* use Leveled Reader practice page 170 to assess their understanding of the Leveled Reader and the target comprehension skill. Additional after reading activities are provided on page 69.

At a Glance

Links to the Student Edition

🎯 **Comprehension Skill:** Main Idea

Selection Vocabulary: *has, going, thank*

Program Theme: Traditions
Unit Theme: Favorite Things Old and New

Some traditions, like the ancient art of karate, are still favorite activities done today.

Before Reading

Motivating the Reader
Build Background About Karate

Ask children if they are familiar with karate. You may want to have volunteers demonstrate typical karate movements. You might also show photographs or a videotape of a karate class. Write *karate* on the chalkboard and read it aloud. Tell children that the word *karate* means "empty hands" in Japanese, and that karate is an ancient way of fighting without weapons. The Japanese, Chinese, Koreans, and Taiwanese all have their own forms of karate. Ask children if they would like to learn how to do karate. Encourage them to give reasons to support their answers.

Preview and Predict

Have children scan the cover, text, and illustrations. Draw children's attention to the book title, and have children tell what they see happening in the pictures. Encourage them to use picture clues and familiar words to predict what the story is about. Encourage them to read to find out what Linn does at karate class.

Point out the selection vocabulary and other unfamiliar words that are important to understanding the book, such as *karate, outfit, chops, pajamas, ready, begin,* and *quiet.*

During Reading

Guiding Comprehension

Use the following questions to support children as they read.

- **Page 2** *Who is this book about?* (a girl named Linn) *What is Linn doing?* (She is getting ready to go to karate class.)

- **Page 3** *Does Linn like going to karate class? How do you know?* (Yes. The words say, "She loves it!")

- **Pages 5–6** *What do you think the colors of the belts mean?* (The colors show how good you are at karate.) *Why does Linn want a black belt?* (A black belt means you are one of the best. Linn wants to be the best.)

- **Pages 6–7** *What can the people who have black belts do?* (They can chop wood with their bare hands.)

- **Page 8** *What does Linn do first in karate class?* (She takes off her shoes.) *What does she do next?* (She bows to her teacher.)

- **Page 9** *What does the bow mean?* (The bow means "I am ready.")

- **Pages 10–11** *What actions does Linn do? What sounds does she make?* (Linn kicks, blocks, hops, and chops. She yells a special karate yell.)

- **Page 12** *Do you think people hurt each other in karate class? How do you know?* (No. It says, "Everyone has fun." It wouldn't be fun if people really got hurt.)

- **Page 13** *What does this bow mean?* (It means "Thank you.")

- **Pages 14–15** *What happens at the end of a karate class?* (Everyone is quiet. Then the students bow to the teacher to say "Thank you for the class.")

- **Page 16** *How does Linn feel after karate?* (She feels good.) *Why do you think she feels like that?* (Answers will vary.)

- **Page 16** *What is the book all about?* (It is all about what happens at Linn's karate class.)

Reading Strategies

If...	Then...
If... a child mistakenly decodes *bow* using the long *o* sound instead,	**Then...** model both ways to say *bow* and have the child decide which word makes the most sense in the sentence.
If... a child has to solve more than one new word on a page,	**Then...** have the child reread the page once or twice, until he or she can read it smoothly.
If... a child has difficulty identifying the book's main idea,	**Then...** use **Model Your Thinking** below.

Model Your Thinking

 Comprehension Skill: Main Idea

Every book is about something. I can use my own words to tell what the book is about. The title of the book tells me that it is about a karate class. I learn something about Linn's karate class on each page, so I know this book is all about Linn's karate class. I see on page 4 that Linn wears a special karate outfit, but this is only a small part of what the whole book is about.

After Reading

Revisiting the Text

Comprehension Write three choices for the book's main idea on the chalkboard. Have small groups reread the book and pick one choice. Have groups explain their choices. Then discuss what children learned about karate. Record their ideas in a large word web drawn on the chalkboard.

16A
Be There!

by Lilly Ernesto
Leveled Reader 16A
Genre: Rhyme
Level: Easy

Summary

A family gets ready and goes to a street fair. Readers get practice telling time as the family goes from one event to another, including a puppet show, a pet show, a ballgame, a pony ride, and a dance.

Leveled Reader Practice

After children have read *Be There!*, use Leveled Reader practice page 171 to assess their understanding of the Leveled Reader and the target comprehension skill. Additional after reading activities are provided on page 71.

At a Glance

Links to the Student Edition

↻ **Comprehension Skill:** Author's Purpose

Selection Vocabulary: *be, pretty, friend*

Program Theme: Traditions
Unit Theme: Favorite Things Old and New

An entire neighborhood is brought together by the traditional sights and smells of a street fair.

Before Reading

Motivating the Reader
Build Background About Fairs and Telling Time

Ask children who have been to fairs to describe their experiences. Have children talk about the kinds of activities and foods one finds at fairs. You may also want to review telling time by setting a clock to different times and then having children tell what time it is. Work together to make an imaginary schedule of what children will do at a fair.

Preview and Predict

Have children scan the cover, text, and illustrations. Draw their attention to the word *clock* and the picture of a clock on page 2. Have children find other examples of clocks or words related to time in the illustrations. Invite a volunteer to read aloud the sign the family is looking at on the book cover. Encourage them to use picture clues and familiar words to predict what the story is about by asking:

> What is this book about? How do you know? Why do you think this book was written?

Then have children set their own purpose for reading, such as reading to find out what the family does at the street fair.

Point out the selection vocabulary and other unfamiliar words that are important to understanding the book, such as *clock, time, seat, slide,* and *stop.*

During Reading

● Guiding Comprehension

Use the following questions to support children as they read.

- **Page 2** *What is the family doing?* (The family is packing a bag. They are getting ready to go somewhere.) *What time is it?* (It is 8 o'clock.)

- **Page 3** *Where do you think the children are now?* (They are at a puppet show at the fair.) *What time is it?* (It is 9 o'clock.) Ask similar questions for each page.

- **Pages 2–3** *There is one word on page 2 that rhymes with a word on page 3. What two words rhyme?* (go and know) Ask similar questions for other pairs of pages until children begin to recognize the rhyming pattern.

- **Pages 4–7** *What do the words and pictures show that you can do at a fair?* (You can have fun with a clown. You can run in a race. You can get food to eat. You can eat in a seat.)

- **Pages 8–9** *What two activities are shown here?* (a pet show and a game of T-ball) *Do these activities take place at the same time or at different times? How do you know?* (They take place at the same time. Both signs say "2–4 P.M.")

- **Page 10** *What time is it now?* (It is 4 o'clock.) *How do you know?* (The sign says "Pony Rides 4 o'clock," and the words say, "It is time to ride." So it must be 4 o'clock.)

- **Page 14** *Why is it time for a friend?* (It is time for a dance, and it's fun to dance with a friend.)

- **Page 15** *What do you think the last page will say? Why?* (The ending on page 16 will rhyme with *friend* because the pages rhyme and the sentence on page 15 isn't finished. Maybe it will say, "The end.")

- **Page 16** *Why do you think the author wrote this book?* (to tell about what happens at a fair; to help readers practice telling time; to write something that is fun to read)

Reading Strategies

If... a child hesitates at the last word on a right-hand page,	**Then...** call attention to the rhyming scheme. Encourage the child to use this relationship to figure out the rhyming word.
If... a child reads smoothly and rhythmically,	**Then...** acknowledge that he or she has mastered the pattern and is reading fluently.
If... a child has difficulty explaining why the author may have written the book,	**Then...** use **Model Your Thinking** below.

Model Your Thinking

☞ **Comprehension Skill: Author's Purpose**

As I read, I think about why the author wrote this book. It happens at a fair, and it shows different things people can do at a fair. It also says, "Look at the clock" on every page, and the pictures show different clocks and signs about time. There are also fun rhymes in the book. I think the author wants the reader to learn how to tell time, and she makes it fun by having the story take place at a fair and by using rhyming words.

After Reading

Revisiting the Text

Comprehension Read the story again with children. Then have children pretend they are the author of the book. Act out an interview by asking children questions about the book, including why the author wrote it.

16B
Zulu Dancer

by Anne Sibley O'Brien
Leveled Reader 16B
Genre: Realistic Story
Level: Easy/Average

Summary

A young African boy wants to be a Zulu dancer like his older brother. He's too young to go with his brother to dance class, but his brother teaches him some steps. The boy dreams that one day soon he too will be a Zulu dancer.

Leveled Reader Practice

After children have read *Zulu Dancer,* use Leveled Reader practice page 172 to assess their understanding of the Leveled Reader and the target comprehension skill. Additional after reading activities are provided on page 73.

At a Glance

Links to the Student Edition

↻ **Comprehension Skill:** Author's Purpose

Selection Vocabulary: *your, soon, be*

Program Theme: Traditions
Unit Theme: Favorite Things Old and New

Carrying on traditions, such as traditional dances, is one way we help keep the past alive and learn about who we are.

Before Reading

Motivating the Reader
Build Background About Dancing

Invite children to describe different kinds of dancing they are familiar with. Ask them when and where these dances have taken place. If possible, show pictures or videotape of different dancing styles and traditions. Encourage children to describe different kinds of traditional dances from their respective cultures.

Preview and Predict

Have children scan the cover, text, and illustrations. Encourage them to use picture clues and familiar words to predict what the story is about by asking:

> **What do you think might happen in this book? Why do you think the author wrote this book?**

Suggest children read to find out what a Zulu dancer is. Point out the selection vocabulary and other unfamiliar words that are important to understanding the book, such as *dancer, dance, may, class, hard, stomp, kick, high,* and *sky.*

During Reading

Guiding Comprehension

Use the following questions to support children as they read.

- **Pages 2–3** Who is telling this story? How do you know? (A young boy is telling the story. He is shown on page 2 and is pointing to his brother who dances.) **Where do you think the boy lives? Why?** (He lives in Africa. I see a map of Africa.)

- **Pages 3–4** How does a Zulu dancer dance? (fast and hard) **What kind of dance steps does a Zulu dancer do?** (A Zulu dancer stomps, jumps, and kicks.)

- **Page 5** Which two words rhyme on this page? (high and sky)

- **Pages 6–7** What does the little boy want? How do you think he feels? (He wants to go to class and become a dancer. I think he feels sad because he can't go to dance class. He looks sad.)

- **Pages 8–9** What does the older brother do? (He helps his younger brother to learn to dance a little.) **Why do you think the brother decides to help?** (He sees how much the little boy wants to be a Zulu dancer.)

- **Page 10** Who is speaking on this page? (The older brother is speaking. He tells his little brother to see how he moves.)

- **Pages 10–11** What is happening? (The older brother shows what a Zulu dancer does. He stomps, jumps, and kicks. The little brother does the same dance steps.)

- **Pages 14–15** What is happening now? (The little boy is in bed, and he imagines himself dancing with other Zulu dancers.)

- **Page 16** Is the boy a Zulu dancer now? How do you know? (No, he is not. He says he *will* be a Zulu dancer, so he isn't one yet.)

- **Page 16** Why do you think the author wrote this book? (to tell about Zulu dancing; to tell an interesting story about an African boy who wants to be a Zulu dancer)

Ongoing Assessment

Reading Strategies

If... a child has difficulty understanding the words *stomp, jump,* and *kick,*	**Then...** demonstrate the words for him or her, and have the child imitate you.
If... a child seems unclear about who is speaking on pages 6–10,	**Then...** explain how the child can tell who is speaking and what is said by looking at the words outside and inside the quotation marks.
If... a child has difficulty explaining why the author may have written the book,	**Then...** use **Model Your Thinking** below.

Model Your Thinking

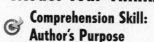

Comprehension Skill: Author's Purpose

As I read, I think about why the author wrote the book. This book is about a boy who wants to be a Zulu dancer. The boy wants to dance so badly that he doesn't take "no" for an answer. He keeps asking until his brother shows him steps from Zulu dancing. The boy does the same steps as his brother and dreams of the day when he will be a Zulu dancer. I think the author wanted to tell about Zulu dancing. I think she also wanted to tell an interesting story about a boy who wants to be a Zulu dancer. I learned something about what this kind of dancing is like, and I enjoyed reading about this boy.

After Reading

Revisiting the Text

Comprehension Discuss the reason or reasons why the author wrote this book. Record children's ideas in Web 2 on page 132. Then have children draw a picture of something they liked about the book.

17A
The Three Bears

by Sharon Fear
Leveled Reader 17A
Genre: Animal Fantasy
Level: Easy

Summary

A brown bear family comes home one day to find an extra bowl, an extra chair, and an extra bed in the house. They even find four other bears asleep in the beds. Oops! The three bears realize they are in the wrong house!

Leveled Reader Practice

After children have read *The Three Bears,* use Leveled Reader practice page 173 to assess their understanding of the Leveled Reader and the target comprehension skill. Additional after reading activities are provided on page 75.

At a Glance

Links to the Student Edition

⌖ **Comprehension Skill:** Plot

Selection Vocabulary: *funny, four, count*

Program Theme: Traditions
Unit Theme: Favorite Things Old and New

This folk tale puts a new spin on a traditional tale. Instead of a visit from Goldilocks, the three bear visit the wrong house!

Before Reading

Motivating the Reader
Build Background About "The Three Bears"

Ask children to retell the familiar folk tale, "Goldilocks and the Three Bears." Volunteers can each tell a sentence. Provide hints or story elements as necessary to complete the story. Prompt children to tell what happens in the beginning, middle, and end of the story.

Preview and Predict

Have children scan the cover, text, and illustrations. Encourage them to use picture clues and familiar words to predict what the story is about. Prepare children for reading by asking:

> **What is this story about? How do you know? How do you think it will end? Why?**

Suggest children read to find out how this version of "The Three Bears" is like and unlike other versions they know.

Point out the selection vocabulary and other unfamiliar words that are important to understanding the book, such as *lived, chairs,* and *began.* You may also wish to review number words before children begin reading.

During Reading

Guiding Comprehension

Use the following questions to support children as they read.

- **Pages 2–3** *How is the beginning of this story like the Goldilocks story? How is it different?* (Both stories begin with three bears. But the three bears' house in the Goldilocks story was in the woods. This one is on a street with other houses.)

- **Page 4** Point to the word *bowls*. *What is this word?* (bowls) *Point to the bowls in the picture.* (Children should point out the three bowls in the picture.)

- **Page 5** *How many chairs are there? How do you know?* (There are three chairs. I see the word *three*, and I can count three chairs in the picture.)

- **Pages 4–5** *What do these three dots after the words mean?* (It means the sentence continues. It is not finished yet.)

- **Pages 7–9** *Why does the little bear say, "That is funny!"?* (When the bears count the number of bowls, there are four bowls, not three.) *What does the word funny mean in this sentence?* (It means "strange, weird.")

- **Page 9** *What do you think will happen next?* (They will count four chairs and four beds.)

- **Pages 10–11** *What happened next?* (The bears counted four chairs and four beds.) *What do you think has happened?* (Maybe the bears are in the wrong house. Maybe another person has moved into their house while they were out.)

- **Page 12** *What do the three bears see?* (They see four bears sleeping in the four beds.)

- **Page 16** *How does the story end?* (The bears realize they are in the wrong house.)

Reading Strategies

If...	Then...
If... a child hesitates when reading but says the right word,	**Then...** ask "What did you notice there that helped you know that word?"
If... a child does not understand that the bears are in the wrong house,	**Then...** have him or her review the illustrations on pages 12–16.
If... a child has trouble describing the book's plot,	**Then...** use **Model Your Thinking** below.

Model Your Thinking

 Comprehension Skill: Plot

Think ALOUD

Events in stories happen in order. Every story has a beginning, middle, and end. In the beginning, I read about three bears who live in a house with three bowls, chairs, and beds. In the middle of the story, the bears come home one day and find that there is something strange in the house. They find four chairs, four bowls, and four beds, instead of three. Then they find four black bears sleeping in the beds. The story ends when the three bears find out that they are in the wrong house.

After Reading

Revisiting the Text

Comprehension Work with children to fill out the Plot/Story Sequence chart on page 134. Have children tell what happens in the beginning, middle, and end of the story. Then have children use the information on the organizer to create a group mural. Provide a large piece of paper and divide it into three sections. Teams of children can illustrate the beginning, middle, and end of the story.

17B

Long Tom

by Robert Newell
Leveled Reader 17B
Genre: Fantasy
Level: Easy/Average

Summary

Long Tom, a scarecrow, watches over the cornfield. He scares away some cows, raccoons, and crows. He soon gets lonely and calls for the animals to come back. The crows pick up Tom and take him on a ride in the sky!

Leveled Reader Practice

After children have read *Long Tom,* use Leveled Reader practice page 174 to assess their understanding of the Leveled Reader and the target comprehension skill. Additional after reading activities are provided on page 77.

At a Glance

Links to the Student Edition

⌖ **Comprehension Skill:** Plot

Selection Vocabulary: *long, watch, were*

Program Theme: Traditions
Unit Theme: Favorite Things Old and New

When a scarecrow decides not to do his job in the traditional way, he gains new friends and a new experience—flying!

Before Reading

Motivating the Reader
Build Background About Scarecrows

Ask children what a scarecrow is, and have them tell of any scarecrows they know from stories or films. Tell them that a scarecrow is literally a figure used to scare away crows and other animals that might eat crops. A scarecrow is often made to look like a person, and has a scarf, arms, and legs that move with the wind and scare the birds. Invite volunteers to draw pictures of scarecrows, act out the motions of a scarecrow, or say something they think a scarecrow would say if it could talk.

Preview and Predict

Have children scan the cover, text, and illustrations. Encourage them to use picture clues and familiar words to predict what the story is about. Prepare children for reading by saying:

> Who is this story about? How can you tell? What do you think might happen? Read to find out what happens to Long Tom.

Point out the selection vocabulary and other unfamiliar words that are important to understanding the book, such as *corn, alone, went, back, flap,* and *no one.*

During Reading

Guiding Comprehension

Use the following questions to support children as they read.

- **Page 2** Who is Long Tom? (a scarecrow) **What is he doing?** (He is watching and protecting a field of corn.)

- **Page 3** Look at Long Tom's face. How do you think he feels? Why does he feel this way? (He is mad because the cows are eating the corn. It is the scarecrow's job to keep animals from eating the food a farmer grows.)

- **Page 5** Who goes away? (the cows) **Why do they go away?** (They were scared away by Long Tom's flapping arms and the noise.)

- **Pages 6–7** Now what does Long Tom see? (He sees raccoons eating the corn.) **What does Long Tom do?** (He scares them away by flapping his arms and making loud noises.)

- **Page 7** What do you think will happen next? (Long Tom will see other animals in the corn, and he will scare them away by flapping his arms.)

- **Pages 8–9** What does Long Tom see? (The crows are eating the corn.) **What does he do?** (Long Tom flaps his arms and scares the crows away.)

- **Pages 10–11** What happens now? How do you think he feels? (Long Tom is all alone. I think he feels lonely.)

- **Pages 12–15** What did Long Tom do? What happened then? (He called for the animals to come back. The animals all came back.)

- **Pages 13–16** What do the animals do to Long Tom? (The cows knock over the pole, the raccoons untie Long Tom, and the crows pick up Long Tom and fly with him.)

- **Page 16** How do you think Long Tom feels now? (Long Tom looks very happy. He is having fun with the animals.)

Reading Strategies

If... a child stops at an unfamiliar word,	Then... ask him or her to read to the end of the sentence and tell what word makes sense in the sentence.
If... a child uses the illustrations to help read unfamiliar words,	Then... praise the child and remind him or her that using the illustrations for clues is a good way to figure out new words.
If... a child has trouble describing the plot,	Then... use **Model Your Thinking** below.

Model Your Thinking

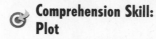 **Comprehension Skill: Plot**

 Think ALOUD

Events in a story happen in an order. Every story has a beginning, middle, and end. At the beginning of the story, I read about Long Tom who is a scarecrow watching the corn. First he scares away the cows. Then he scares the raccoons and the crows. In the middle of the story, Long Tom begins to feel lonely because he is now all alone. So he calls for the animals to come back. At the end of the story, the crows pick up Long Tom and carry him away. Long Tom is happy to have friends, and he likes flying.

After Reading

Revisiting the Text

Comprehension Have pairs reread the book and fill out the Plot/Story Sequence organizer on page 134. Children can draw or write what happens in the beginning, middle, and end of the story. Then encourage children to use their charts and take turns retelling the story to their partners.

18A
Knock-Knock Jokes

by Phoebe Marsh
Leveled Reader 18A
Genre: Humorous Story
Level: Easy

Summary

A young chimpanzee's mother and father tell him a series of knock-knock jokes, all having to do with fruit. The young chimp responds with his own joke about making fruit salad.

Leveled Reader Practice

After children have read *Knock-Knock Jokes,* use Leveled Reader practice page 175 to assess their understanding of the Leveled Reader and the target comprehension skill. Additional after reading activities are provided on page 79.

At a Glance

Links to the Student Edition

☞ **Comprehension Skill:** Realism and Fantasy

Selection Vocabulary: *answer, ask, kind*

Program Theme: Traditions
Unit Theme: Favorite Things Old and New

An old favorite, the knock-knock joke, gets a new twist when told by a family of chimpanzees.

Before Reading

Motivating the Reader

Build Background About Knock-Knock Jokes

Ask children if they know what knock-knock jokes are, and have them share any jokes they know. If children can't think of examples, tell some yourself. For example, "Knock-knock." "Who is there?" "Radio." "Radio who?" "Radio not, here I come." "Knock-knock." "Who is there?" "Lettuce." "Lettuce who?" "Lettuce in and we'll tell you more knock-knock jokes." Point out that you need to pay attention to the words in a knock-knock joke because they are often used in a funny way.

Preview and Predict

Have children scan the cover, text, and illustrations. Encourage them to use picture clues and familiar words to predict whether the story is real or make-believe and what the story is about. Then have children set their own purpose for reading, such as reading to find out what knock-knock jokes the little chimpanzee will tell.

Point out the selection vocabulary and other unfamiliar words that are important to understanding the book, such as *knock, joke,* and *salad.* Draw children's attention to compound words, such as *blueberry,* and encourage children to look for smaller words in these longer words to help them read the compound words.

During Reading

Guiding Comprehension

Use the following questions to support children as they read.

- **Page 2** *Do you think the story will tell about something real or make-believe? How do you know?* (It is a make-believe story because chimpanzees don't talk or live in houses like real people do.)

- **Page 2** *What does the little chimpanzee want his parents to do?* (He wants them to ask him some knock-knock jokes.)

- **Pages 3–4** *Who asks the first joke? How can you tell?* (The father chimpanzee asks the first joke. The speech balloons tell who is talking, and I read the words from top to bottom.)

- **Page 4** Point to *blueberry*. *What two smaller words do you see in this long word?* (blue and berry) Ask similar questions about other compound words.

- **Pages 5–6** *Who asks the next joke?* (The mother chimpanzee asks the next joke.)

- **Page 7** *What do you think the next joke will be about? Why do you think that?* (The next one will be about fruit too. The first two jokes were about fruit.)

- **Page 9** *What kind of fruit do you think the next joke will be about? How do you know?* (It will be about an orange. The little chimpanzee is drawing a picture of an orange.)

- **Page 13** *What do you think the next knock-knock joke will be about? What do you think the answer might be? How can you tell?* (It will be about a strawberry, and the answer is strawberry jam. I see the painting of a strawberry and I see a jar of jam with a strawberry on it.)

- **Page 16** *What does the little chimp want to make?* (He wants to make fruit salad.)

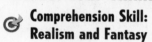
Reading Strategies

If... a child has difficulty making accurate predictions,	**Then...** point out that the little chimpanzee's drawings are story clues.
If... a child has trouble following the dialogue,	**Then...** suggest that he or she track the words with a finger, and then track the balloon pointer to find who the speaker is.
If... a child has difficulty with the new fruit words and joke answers,	**Then...** guide him or her to use picture clues and break apart compound words to figure out the words.
If... a child cannot tell that the story is make-believe,	**Then...** use **Model Your Thinking** below.

Model Your Thinking

🔁 **Comprehension Skill: Realism and Fantasy**

Some stories tell only about things that could really happen. Make-believe stories tell about things that couldn't really happen. This story is about a chimpanzee family that tells knock-knock jokes. I know that chimpanzees cannot talk. They also do not usually wear clothes, live in a house, or bake. So I know this story is make-believe. Make-believe stories sometimes include things that could really happen. For example, all the different foods shown are real kinds of food.

After Reading

Revisiting the Text

Comprehension Ask children if this story is real or make-believe. Discuss why the story is make-believe. Then have groups reread the story and think about what parts of the story could really happen and which parts couldn't really happen. Children can write words or draw pictures in the T-Chart on page 140.

18B
The First Day of Winter

by Gordon L. Storey
Leveled Reader 18B
Genre: Animal Fantasy
Level: Easy/Average

Summary

One snowy winter day, little Bunny decides to go outside and play. His mother tells him to dress warmly. She has Little Bunny put on four shirts, three pairs of pants, three sweaters, six socks, four mittens, a hat, a scarf, and boots. But now Bunny can't go outside. He has fallen over because he is wearing too many clothes. He can't get up!

Leveled Reader Practice

After children have read *The First Day of Winter,* use Leveled Reader practice page 176 to assess their understanding of the Leveled Reader and the target comprehension skill. Additional after reading activities are provided on page 81.

At a Glance

Links to the Student Edition

⌖ **Comprehension Skill:** Realism and Fantasy

Selection Vocabulary: *about, any, over*

Program Theme: Traditions
Unit Theme: Favorite Things Old and New

Playing in the snow is a traditionally favorite pastime—that is, if you can get out the door!

Before Reading

Motivating the Reader
Build Background About Winter

Tell children that the story they will read takes place during the winter. Ask,

> What does winter feel like?
> What clothes would you wear to
> keep warm and dry? What is fun to
> do in wintry weather?

Have children draw pictures of themselves doing something outside in the snow. Help them label the different items in their pictures, such as snow, sled, hat, scarf, mittens, and so on.

Preview and Predict

Have children scan the cover, text, and illustrations. Encourage them to use picture clues and familiar words to predict what the story is about. Prepare children for reading by saying:

> What do you think Bunny likes to
> do in winter? What will Bunny need
> to do before going outside? Read to
> find out what happens to Bunny.

Point out the selection vocabulary and other unfamiliar words that are important to understanding the book, such as *winter, much, let's, dress, warm, any,* and *can't.*

During Reading

Guiding Comprehension

Use the following questions to support children as they read.

- **Page 2** Do you think this story tells about something that could really happen, or is it make-believe? How do you know? (It is make-believe because rabbits don't talk, wear clothes, or live in a house as real people do.)

- **Page 2** What time of year is it? How do you know? (It is winter. I see the snow outside and I read the word *winter*. The book is called *The First Day of Winter*.)

- **Pages 2–3** What does Bunny want to do? (He wants to go play in the snow.) What does his mother tell him to do before they can go out? (She tells him to dress warm.)

- **Page 4** Who is asking this question? (Mama asks this question. She answers it before Bunny can speak.)

- **Pages 4–5** What does Bunny put on first? (He puts on shirts.) How many shirts does he put on? (four)

- **Pages 6–7** What does Bunny put on next? (He puts on pants.) How many pairs of pants does he put on? (three pairs of pants)

- **Pages 8–12** What other clothes does Mama ask Bunny to put on? (three sweaters, six thick socks, four fat mittens)

- **Page 13** What does Bunny say each time his mother tells him to put on clothes? (He says, "I can do that.")

- **Page 13** How do you think Bunny feels? How do you know? (I think he feels very hot. He is inside and has on so many clothes! He looks as if he's sweating!)

- **Pages 14–15** Why do you think Bunny says he can't go out? (Possible answer: He can't move because he is wearing so many clothes.)

- **Page 16** Why can't Bunny go out? (He has on so many clothes that he has fallen over. He can't get up.)

Reading Strategies

If... a child hesitates before unfamiliar clothing words,

Then... encourage him or her to use knowledge of sounds and letters to figure out a word, and then check it against the illustrations.

If... a child makes good predictions based on story events and sentence patterns,

Then... praise the child for using what has happened so far to tell what might come next.

If... a child can't tell that this is a make-believe story,

Then... use **Model Your Thinking** below.

Model Your Thinking

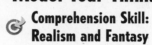

Comprehension Skill: Realism and Fantasy

Think ALOUD

As I read, I ask myself: "Does this story tell about something that could happen in real life? Or is it a make-believe story?" In the first picture, I see Bunny and his Mama dressed in clothes in a living room. Real rabbits don't have homes like that. They don't wear clothes. They can't talk. So I know this story is make-believe. Make-believe stories tell about things that couldn't really happen. Some make-believe stories also have parts that could really happen. For example, most mothers usually make you dress very warm before you go out in the snow. If I put on all those clothes, I would feel too hot and have a hard time moving, just like Bunny.

After Reading

Revisiting the Text

Comprehension Discuss whether this story is about something real or make-believe. Then have partners reread the book and use the T-Chart on page 140 to write words or draw pictures to show which parts of the story could really happen and which parts couldn't really happen. Have children share their charts and tell which part of the story they liked the best.

19A
That Is Right, Walrus

by Kana Riley
Leveled Reader 19A
Genre: Animal Fantasy
Level: Easy

Summary

Walrus is planning trips to the beach, a ranch, camping, and a visit to Grandma. She needs to figure out what is the correct thing to buy for each trip. For example, she wonders whether to buy a snowsuit or a bathing suit for a trip to the beach. Readers learn the correct choice for each trip. When it comes to getting a gift for her Grandma, Walrus discovers both ideas are right.

Leveled Reader Practice

After children have read *That Is Right, Walrus,* use Leveled Reader practice page 177 to assess their understanding of the Leveled Reader and the target comprehension skill. Additional after reading activities are provided on page 83.

At a Glance

Links to the Student Edition

⌖ **Comprehension Skill:** Predicting

Selection Vocabulary: *buy, or, right*

Program Theme: Journeys in Time and Space
Unit Theme: Take Me There

Going on a journey requires careful planning so you will be well prepared.

Before Reading

Motivating the Reader
Build Background About Packing for a Trip

Ask children to think of a trip they have taken. It could be a trip to a faraway place or a visit to someone nearby. Encourage children to talk about their travels. Guide them to relate the things they took with them to the needs of the trip. Then play a guessing game. Say:

> I'm going to the desert. Which will I need, a hair dryer or a water bottle?

Have the child who answers correctly make up another question.

Preview and Predict

Have children scan the cover, text, and illustrations to get an idea of what the book is about. Prepare children for reading by saying:

> Walrus needs help choosing what to take with her on some trips. As you read, try to think about what might happen if she makes the wrong choice. Then decide what is the right choice.

Draw pictures and write labels for each of Walrus's choices in the T-Chart on page 140. Give each child a copy. As they read, children can circle the choice or choices they predict will be the right choice. Encourage them to read to find out if their predictions are correct.

Point out selection vocabulary and any unfamiliar words that are important to understanding the book, such as *walrus, beach, ranch,* and *camping.*

During Reading

Guiding Comprehension

Use the following questions to support children as they read.

- **Page 2** **Where is Walrus going?** (She is going to the beach.)

- **Page 3** **What two things is Walrus thinking of buying?** (She is buying either a snowsuit or a bathing suit.) **Which do you think is the better choice? Why?** (The bathing suit is the better choice because it is hot at the beach and you can swim there.)

- **Pages 4–5** **Why is the snowsuit not a good choice for this trip?** (The snowsuit is too hot for the beach.)

- **Pages 6–13** Ask similar questions as those above for each set of choices. Encourage children to use the story pattern to predict which choice is the best one.

- **Pages 14–15** **Where is Walrus going now?** (She is going to see her grandmother.) **What two things is Walrus thinking of buying?** (She is buying either a book or flowers.) **Which do you think Walrus will choose?** (Answers will vary. Some children will choose either the book or the flowers, and some may choose both.)

- **Page 16** **What did Walrus buy for her grandmother?** (She bought both a book and flowers.)

- **Page 16** **When you are planning to buy something for a trip, what things should you think about to help you figure out what to buy?** (Answers will vary. Possible answers include: temperature, weather, activities you can do, size of your suitcase or backpack)

Reading Strategies

If... a child hesitates before *beach*, *ranch*, or *camping*,	Then... support the child in using sound-letter knowledge and picture clues to figure out the word. Do the same with the items Walrus may buy.
If... a child skims over the "No, no," and "Yes, Walrus!" pages, saying the words from memory,	Then... have the child slow down and read with a finger to track the words.
If... a child had difficulty making accurate predictions,	Then... use **Model Your Thinking** below.

Model Your Thinking

Comprehension Skill: Predicting

As I read this book, it helps to think about what will happen next in the story. Walrus is going to the beach, and she has to choose what to take. She is thinking of buying a snowsuit or a bathing suit. I know beaches are hot, so buying a snowsuit isn't a good idea. I also know you can swim at a beach, so buying a bathing suit is a good idea. I keep reading to see if I was right. As I continue to read, I will think about what Walrus will buy for each of her trips. Thinking about each choice is a good way for me to tell what will happen next.

After Reading

Revisiting the Text

Comprehension Have children share the predictions they circled on the T-Charts while reading. Discuss what clues children used to decide which choice or choices were right. Have pairs extend the story by showing another trip Walrus will take.

19B
Texas Eggs

by Sydnie Meltzer Kleinhenz
Leveled Reader 19B
Genre: Realistic Story
Level: Easy/Average

Summary

A young girl visits her grandpa in Texas. Each day they eat eggs, and Grandpa saves the shells. Each day the girl asks why, but Grandpa won't tell her. When they have a party, the girl learns that Grandpa has filled the eggshells with confetti. They have fun breaking the eggs over each other's heads.

Leveled Reader Practice

After children have read *Texas Eggs,* use Leveled Reader practice page 178 to assess their understanding of the Leveled Reader and the target comprehension skill. Additional after reading activities are provided on page 85.

At a Glance

Links to the Student Edition

☞ **Comprehension Skill:** Predicting

Selection Vocabulary: *only, think*

Program Theme: Journeys in Time and Space
Unit Theme: Take Me There

It's always fun to travel and visit loved ones.

Before Reading

Motivating the Reader
Build Background About Visiting Grandparents

Ask children if they have ever visited a grandparent or other relative. Encourage them to tell whom they visited, where they traveled, and how they got there. Ask them to share special things that they did with their grandparents or relatives.

Preview and Predict

Have children scan the cover, text, and illustrations. Encourage them to use picture clues and familiar words to predict what the story is about. Prepare children for reading by saying:

> Where is the girl going? Whom is she visiting? What do you think she will learn about? As you read, pay attention to what the girl's grandfather does with the eggs.

As children read, encourage them to use the T-Chart on page 140 to record their predictions of what will happen next. They can write page numbers in the left column and draw pictures or write words to show their predictions in the right column.

Point out selection vocabulary and any unfamiliar words that are important to understanding the book, such as *Texas, Grandpa, eggs, shells,* and *party.*

During Reading

Guiding Comprehension

Use the following questions to support children as they read.

- **Pages 2–3** *Where is the girl going?* (She is going to Texas.) *Who is she visiting?* (She is visiting her grandfather.) *How does she get to Texas? How do you know?* (She flies in an airplane. I know because there is a sign that says, "Flight 360 from New York." Also there is a plane taking off in the background.)

- **Page 4** *How does the girl feel about visiting her grandpa?* (She likes being with him because he is funny.)

- **Page 6** *Where did the shells come from?* (They are the eggshells left over from the eggs the girl and her grandfather ate.)

- **Pages 6–7** *What does the girl ask her grandpa?* (She wants to know why he is keeping the eggshells.) *What is his answer?* (He says the shells are only for fun, and he puts one on his nose like a clown.)

- **Page 9** *What do you think will happen next? Why?* (They will eat more eggs. Grandpa will save the eggshells. When his granddaughter asks why, he will say, "Only for fun." This pattern has already happened twice, so I think it will happen again.)

- **Page 13** *Why do you think the grandfather is saving the eggshells?* (Answers will vary.)

- **Pages 14–15** *What is the grandfather doing? What do you think he will do with the eggs now?* (Grandpa is filling an eggshell with confetti. I think he will break the shells, and the confetti will come out.)

- **Page 16** *How do the girl and her grandpa play with eggs?* (When they break the eggs, colorful confetti falls out.)

Reading Strategies

If... a child reads slowly and with difficulty,	Then... call attention to the sentence pattern that starts on pages 6–7. Have the child note where the pattern recurs in the text.
If... a child has difficulty making accurate predictions,	Then... use **Model Your Thinking** below.

Model Your Thinking

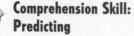 Comprehension Skill: Predicting

As I read this book, I keep wondering what will happen next. I think about what has happened already to try to figure out what will happen next. On page 5, when the girl says they eat eggs, I wonder why she tells us that. On page 7, I notice that Grandpa looks at her, and gives an answer that doesn't tell very much. "Only for fun," he says. What does that mean? On page 15, I can see that he is putting confetti, tiny colorful pieces of paper, in the eggs. I've seen people throw confetti at parties, and I know the characters are having a party. I predict that the eggs are for the party, maybe to break and get confetti over everyone. I read to see if I'm right. On page 16, the girl finally gets to play with the eggs herself and throw confetti all over Grandpa.

After Reading

Revisiting the Text

Comprehension Have children share the T-Charts they completed to show the predictions they made while reading. Invite volunteers to read the book aloud. Have children tell the predictions they made as each page is read.

20A
From Dad

by Dona R. McDuff
Leveled Reader 20A
Genre: Realistic Story
Level: Easy

Summary

A girl treasures a T-shirt that she receives from her dad. When she was little, the shirt was too big. But she wore it anyway. Then she was six and it fit just right. Now she is seven and the shirt is too small. Her dad gives her a new T-shirt. She finds a way to keep and use both the old T-shirt and the new one.

Leveled Reader Practice

After children have read *From Dad,* use Leveled Reader practice page 179 to assess their understanding of the Leveled Reader and the target comprehension skill. Additional after reading activities are provided on page 87.

At a Glance

Links to the Student Edition

🖝 **Comprehension Skill:** Compare and Contrast

Selection Vocabulary: *don't, from, hear*

Program Theme: Journeys in Time and Space
Unit Theme: Take Me There

As we grow, some things, like favorite T-shirts, don't grow with us, but we still think they are special.

Before Reading

Motivating the Reader
Build Background About Favorite Clothes

Ask children to name a favorite item of clothing that they have had for a long time and tell a story about it. Have them describe what the item was like when it was new and what it is like now. Ask them why this item is special to them. Talk about how one feels about something old and dear and how it feels when it's too old or too small to wear. Ask if it is easy to throw such a thing away.

Preview and Predict

Have children scan the cover, text, and illustrations. Encourage them to use picture clues and familiar words to predict what the story is about. Prepare children for reading by saying:

> What do you think the story is about? Follow the girl through the story to see what happens to her. What do you think the girl's problem is?

Suggest children read to find out what problem the girl has and how she solves it.

Point out selection vocabulary and any unfamiliar words that are important to understanding the book, such as *T-shirt, years, looked, school, bigger, smaller,* and *give.*

During Reading

Guiding Comprehension

Use the following questions to support children as they read.

- **Pages 2–3** *What does the girl tell us about her T-shirt?* (She got the T-shirt from her father. She got it when she was little, and the shirt was big and long.)

- **Pages 4–6** *Where did the girl wear her shirt?* (on her swing, at the beach, in bed) *Do you see any patterns in the words?* (Yes. The last two sentences are the same on pages 4–6: "I was little. The shirt looked big.")

- **Page 7** *What happens when the girl turns six years old?* (She has grown bigger, so it made her shirt look smaller.) *Did the shirt really get smaller? How do you know?* (No. It stayed the same size, but the girl grew bigger. The word *looked* is a clue, and I know children outgrow their clothes as they grow bigger.)

- **Pages 8–9** *How did the girl's shirt fit her when she was six?* (It fit just right.)

- **Pages 8–10** *Now where does the girl wear her shirt?* (on her bike, at school, in a tree)

- **Page 11** *How old is the girl now?* (She is seven.) *How does her shirt fit now?* (It is too small for her.)

- **Pages 12–13** *What does the girl's father give her?* (He gives her a new T-shirt.)

- **Pages 14–15** *Does the girl want the new shirt? Why or why not?* (No. She does not want the new shirt. She likes her old shirt.)

- **Page 16** *What does the girl do with her old shirt?* (She puts it on her stuffed bear.) *Do you think this is a good solution to her problem? Why or why not?* (Yes. The girl can still keep and enjoy seeing the old T-shirt, and she can wear and learn to like the new one.)

Reading Strategies

If... a child hesitates on page 4 at *looked*,	**Then...** cover the suffix with your finger. Ask the child to read the base word first, and then add the *-ed*.
If... a child pronounces *give* on page 14 with a long *i* sound instead of a short *i* sound,	**Then...** have him or her read the entire sentence to determine the correct pronunciation.
If... a child has difficulty comparing and contrasting,	**Then...** use **Model Your Thinking** below.

Model Your Thinking

 Comprehension Skill: Compare and Contrast

This is a story about a girl and her favorite T-shirt. As I read about the girl when she was five, six, and then seven years old, I can tell how things are alike and different each year. One way things are alike is that the girl likes to wear her favorite T-shirt. However, as she grew, the shirt didn't fit as well. She is little at five years old but she is bigger at six and even bigger at seven. This is one way she is different each year. At five, the shirt is too big. At six, it is just right. At seven, it is too small. This is how the fit of the shirt is different each year.

After Reading

Revisiting the Text

Comprehension Have pairs reread the book and record details about the girl at ages five, six, and seven in a three-column chart, one column for each age. Have children draw pictures and/or write words about the girl's size, shirt, activities, and feelings. Have pairs use their charts to make statements about how things are alike and different among the ages.

20B

House of Wood, House of Snow

by Barbara Gannett
Leveled Reader 20B
Genre: Narrative Nonfiction
Level: Easy/Average

Summary

A child narrator enjoys living in two kinds of houses—a traditional wood house and an igloo. She points out similarities between the two dwellings. They both have windows and doors, lamps and beds. Perhaps most importantly, they can both be full of friends.

Leveled Reader Practice

After children have read *House of Wood, House of Snow,* use Leveled Reader practice page 180 to assess their understanding of the Leveled Reader and the target comprehension skill. Additional after reading activities are provided on page 89.

At a Glance

Links to the Student Edition

↻ **Comprehension Skill:** Compare and Contrast

Selection Vocabulary: *live, when*

Program Theme: Journeys in Time and Space
Unit Theme: Take Me There

People who live in places with lots of snow build igloos to house visiting guests.

Before Reading

Motivating the Reader
Build Background About Igloos

Ask children to imagine they are out on a snowy day. There's nothing around but snow, snow, snow. Ask them whether they think they could make a house out of the snow. Invite a volunteer to show how he or she would do it. Encourage children to think about how they might build a house of snow and how they could use it. Use reference sources or the Leveled Reader book to show children examples of igloos.

Preview and Predict

Have students scan the cover, text, and illustrations. Encourage them to use picture clues and familiar words to make a prediction of what the story is about. Prepare students for reading by asking:

> The first word in this story is "I," so someone is telling the story. Look through the book. Who is telling the story? How do you know?

Suggest children read to find out how houses made of wood are like and unlike houses made of snow.

Point out selection vocabulary and any unfamiliar words, such as *igloo, door,* and *window,* that might be important to understanding the book.

During Reading

● Guiding Comprehension

Use the following questions to support children as they read.

- **Pages 2–3** Look at these pictures. What do they show about where the people in this story live? (They live where it is very cold. They live in different kinds of houses.)

- **Pages 4–5** How are the windows in the houses alike? How are they different? (Both are used for seeing out. The window in the wood house is a rectangle. The igloo window looks like one half of a circle.)

- **Pages 5–6** How are the doors in the houses alike? How are they different? (Both can be used to get in and out of the houses. The wood house has a wooden door with a window in it. The igloo has a door made of snow. The shape of each door is different.)

- **Pages 7–8** What do you use lamps and beds for? (You use lamps for light and beds for sleeping.)

- **Pages 12–13** Why do you think the girl and her family make igloos when Grandpa or friends visit? (They are used as guest rooms.)

- **Pages 14–15** What does this story tell you about how igloos are made? Where can you find that information? (They are made from blocks of snow, piled in a circle that gets smaller at the top. The picture shows that.)

- **Page 15** There are two words in this book that the author uses when she tells how the houses are alike. One is always at the beginning of a sentence. The other is always at the end of a sentence. What are the words? (both, too)

- **Page 16** How does the girl feel about the two kinds of houses? (She likes both of them.) Do you think you would like to visit the girl and stay in an igloo? Why or why not? (It might be fun to stay in such a different house. It might be awkward getting in and out of the low door.)

Reading Strategies

If... a child reads *live* on page 2 with a long *i* sound instead of a short *i* sound,	Then... ask him or her to read the sentence again and discuss its meaning.
If... a child reads the question on page 12 with proper intonation,	Then... praise him or her for recognizing that the sentence is a question.
If... a child has difficulty comparing and contrasting,	Then... use **Model Your Thinking** below.

Model Your Thinking

 Comprehension Skill: Compare and Contrast

Think
ALOUD

This book is about two kinds of houses—a wood house and an igloo. In some ways, the two houses are the same, or alike. In other ways, they are different. As I read, I look for clues that tell me how the houses are alike and how they are different. On pages 6 and 7, I read that a wood house has a door and an igloo has a door too. That is one way they are alike. The word *too* at the end of a sentence is a clue that the sentence tells about how two things are alike. I also read that one of the doors is made of wood. The other is made of snow. That's a way the houses are different. Thinking about the ways the houses are alike and different helps me understand more about them.

After Reading

Revisiting the Text

Comprehension Ask pairs to reread the book. Have them use the T-Chart on page 140 to show how the two houses are alike and different. Have children draw the wood house on the left side and the igloo on the right. Children can use their charts as a prop and point out similarities and differences between the houses.

21A
Mary Goes Walking

by Anne Phillips
Leveled Reader 21A
Genre: Realistic Story
Level: Easy

Summary

Little Mary plays dress up—putting on a pair of shoes, a dress, and a hat—and then goes walking outside. She comes to a puddle and admires her reflection in it. As she leans over to see more of her reflection, she falls in the puddle. In her wet clothes, Mary walks all the way home.

Leveled Reader Practice

After children have read *Mary Goes Walking,* use Leveled Reader practice page 181 to assess their understanding of the Leveled Reader and the target comprehension skill. Additional after reading activities are provided on page 91.

At a Glance

Links to the Student Edition

◔ **Comprehension Skill:** Sequence

Selection Vocabulary: *her, new, show*

Program Theme: Journeys in Time and Space
Unit Theme: Take Me There

Even the shortest of journeys, such as a walk down the street, can have unexpected results.

Before Reading

Motivating the Reader
Build Background About New Clothes

Ask children what they do when they get new clothes. Ask them if they put them in a drawer or if they put them on and wear them right away. Discuss how they feel wearing new clothes. Invite children to pantomime opening a bag or box containing two items of new clothes, putting them on, and showing them off, as Mary does in the story.

Preview and Predict

Have children scan the cover, text, and illustrations. Encourage them to use picture clues and familiar words to predict what the story is about. Prepare children for reading by saying:

> Who is this story about? Why do you think Mary goes walking? Read to find out what happens during her walk.

Point out selection vocabulary and any unfamiliar words that are important to understanding the book, such as *off, next, leans, sees,* and *wet.*

During Reading

Guiding Comprehension

Use the following questions to support children as they read.

- **Page 2** *What is Mary doing?* (She is putting on a pair of new blue shoes.)

- **Pages 2–3** *What does Mary show off first?* (She shows off her new shoes.) *What color are her shoes?* (They are blue.) *Do you think the shoes are Mary's? Why or why not?* (Possible answers: Yes. They are Mary's shoes because it says "Mary has new shoes." No. They are not Mary's shoes because they are too big and do not fit her feet.)

- **Pages 4–5** *What happens next?* (Mary puts on and shows off her new red dress.)

- **Page 5** *What do you think will happen next?* (Possible answers: She will put on and show off something else new. She will play or go walking in her new clothes.)

- **Pages 6–7** *What does Mary show off now?* (Mary shows off her new hat.) *What color is the hat?* (The hat is yellow.)

- **Pages 8–9** *How do you think Mary feels in her new clothes? How can you tell?* (Mary feels proud of her new clothes. I can tell by her smile and by the way she walks. She enjoys looking at herself in the puddle.)

- **Pages 10–11** *Why do you think Mary leans over?* (She leans over to see more of herself and her new clothes in the water.) *What does she see next?* (She sees her red dress next.)

- **Page 11** *What do you think will happen next?* (She will lean over some more, so she can see her new blue shoes.)

- **Page 13** *What do you think will happen next?* (Possible answers: Maybe she will continue on her walk. Mary will lean over too far and fall in the water.)

- **Page 16** *Now how do you think Mary feels? Why?* (Possible answers: She feels sad because her new clothes are wet. She feels silly because she fell in the water.)

Reading Strategies

If... a child has difficulty with new clothing and color words,	**Then...** support the child in working through the page slowly, using letter-sound knowledge and picture clues.
If... a child hesitates on page 8 at the word *walking*,	**Then...** cover the inflected ending. Have the child read the base word first, add the suffix, and then read the whole sentence.
If... a child has difficulty following the sequence of events,	**Then...** use **Model Your Thinking** below.

Model Your Thinking

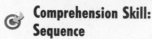 **Comprehension Skill: Sequence**

Think ALOUD

Good readers pay attention to the order in which things happen in a story. I look for clue words such as *first, next, then,* and *finally* to figure out the order of events. In this story, Mary first puts on her blue shoes. Next she puts on the dress. Then she puts on a hat. Then she goes walking. She sees a puddle. The first thing Mary sees in the puddle is her hat. Next she sees her dress. She sees her shoes last. Finally, Mary falls in the puddle and walks home with her wet clothes.

After Reading

Revisiting the Text

Comprehension Help children use the Time Line on page 136 to record the sequence of story events. They can draw pictures and/or write words to show the order of events. Then ask questions about the book using clue words such as *first, next,* and *then.* Children can use their charts to answer the questions.

21B
Desert Fox

by Nat Gabriel
Leveled Reader 21B
Genre: Narrative Nonfiction
Level: Easy/Average

Summary

In the desert of North Africa, a small desert fox sleeps to avoid the scorching heat of the sun. At night, when it is cooler, she comes out to hunt and finds a small lizard to eat.

Leveled Reader Practice

After children have read *Desert Fox,* use Leveled Reader practice page 182 to assess their understanding of the Leveled Reader and the target comprehension skill. Additional after reading activities are provided on page 93.

At a Glance

Links to the Student Edition

↻ **Comprehension Skill:** Sequence

Selection Vocabulary: *old, around*

Program Theme: Journeys in Time and Space
Unit Theme: Take Me There

Stories can take us to faraway places that we've never been before. This book takes readers to a hot desert to see how a desert fox lives.

Before Reading

Motivating the Reader
Build Background About Deserts

Display books with photographs of deserts and desert animals, including the North African desert. Ask children what they think a desert is like. Record their responses in a word web on the chalkboard. Explain, if necessary, that deserts are usually hot during the day, but cool at night.

Preview and Predict

Have children scan the cover, text, and illustrations. Encourage them to use picture clues and familiar words to predict what the story is about. Prepare children for reading by saying:

> What kind of animal is this book about? Where does it live? What does it do? As you read, notice when the fox goes hunting and when she rests.

Point out selection vocabulary and any unfamiliar words that are important to understanding the book, such as *needs, finds, food, hunt, wakes, lizard, hides,* and *waits.*

During Reading

Guiding Comprehension

Use the following questions to support children as they read.

- **Pages 2–3** *What do you see in this desert?* (The sun is coming up. There are a few plants growing in the sand. I see a fox peeking out of a hole.)

- **Pages 4–5** *Why do you think the fox is hot?* (She is hot because the sun is out and it is very hot in the desert.)

- **Page 6** *Why does the fox need water?* (She is thirsty. She needs to find water to drink.)

- **Page 7** *What food does the fox find?* (a lizard)

- **Page 8** *Why doesn't the fox hunt now?* (It is too hot to run after the lizard.)

- **Page 9** *What kind of spot does the fox find? How do you know?* (She finds a dark spot out of the sun. The picture shows she is in a dark place.)

- **Pages 10–11** *What time of day is it now? How do you know?* (It is evening. The sun is going down.) *Why does the fox come out now?* (The fox comes out because it is cooler and she can hunt more easily.)

- **Pages 12–13** *How does the fox find the lizard?* (She uses her ears and eyes to find the lizard.)

- **Pages 13–15** *What does she do to catch the lizard?* (First she hides. Then she looks and waits. Next she runs after it. Then she jumps on it, catching it under her paw.)

- **Page 16** *What time is it now? What will the fox do?* (It is morning again. The fox will eat the lizard and then probably rest.)

Reading Strategies

If... a child successfully reads an unknown word,	**Then...** praise him or her and ask what clues he or she used to help figure out the word.
If... a child has difficulty following the sequence of events,	**Then...** use **Model Your Thinking** below.

Model Your Thinking

 Comprehension Skill: Sequence

Think ALOUD

Good readers pay attention to the order in which things happen in a story. I can use clue words such as first, next, and then to help me figure out the order of events. This story begins when the sun comes up. So it is daytime. The fox comes out and looks around. She drinks water. But it is too hot to hunt. She finds a cool place and sleeps. When the sun goes down and night comes, the fox wakes up and goes out. Now it is cool and she can hunt. When she sees the lizard, the first thing she does is hide. Then she looks and waits. Next she runs after it, and then jumps on it. At the end of the night, as the sun is rising, the fox takes the lizard back to her burrow to eat.

After Reading

Revisiting the Text

Comprehension Have children reread pages 13–15 and use clue words to list the sequence of events in the Sequence Chart on page 139. Children can use their charts to act out the fox hunting. Then conduct a book walk, inviting volunteers to tell what happens first, next, and at the end of the story.

22A
All Together Now!

by Susan Hood
Leveled Reader 22A
Genre: Realistic Story
Level: Easy

Summary

A family of five sets out together on a walk. They see a deer, a hawk, many bugs, a cave, and even a bat. They are interested in some paw prints until they discover the animal is a skunk! They quickly run away—together.

Leveled Reader Practice

After children have read *All Together Now!*, use Leveled Reader practice page 183 to assess their understanding of the Leveled Reader and the target comprehension skill. Additional after reading activities are provided on page 95.

At a Glance

Links to the Student Edition

Comprehension Skill: Cause and Effect

Selection Vocabulary: *together, start*

Program Theme: Journeys in Time and Space
Unit Theme: Take Me There

Exploring the natural world around us can be more enjoyable when it's done as a family.

Before Reading

Motivating the Reader
Build Background About Hikes

Ask children if they have gone on a hike or for a walk in the woods. Invite children to share their experiences, telling what they brought with them and how they dressed. Ask what animals they saw. Then invite children to imagine they are setting off on a walk in some hills and woods. Have them imagine and describe the plants, animals, and other natural features they will see.

Preview and Predict

Have children scan the cover, text, and illustrations. Encourage them to use picture clues and familiar words to predict what the story is about. Prepare children for reading by saying:

> Who is going on a walk in this book? What do you think they mean by "All together now!"? Read to find out what adventure they have.

Point out selection vocabulary and any unfamiliar words that are important to understanding the book, such as *family, bright, climb, deep, brave,* and *tracks.*

During Reading

Guiding Comprehension

Use the following questions to support children as they read.

- **Page 2** *Who are these people? What are they doing?* (They are a family going for a walk.)

- **Page 3** *Why are the children pointing?* (They see a hawk in the sky.) *What other animal did they see?* (They saw a deer.)

- **Page 4** *How did the family get wet?* (They got wet crossing a stream.)

- **Page 5** *How do the hugs make the family feel? How do you know?* (The hugs make them feel good. They are smiling. I know I feel good when I give or get a hug.)

- **Page 5** *What do you think they mean when they say, "All together now!"?* (They mean that they are taking this walk together as a family.)

- **Page 6** *What are the parents doing?* (They are slapping at bugs.) *Why do you think they are doing this?* (The bugs may be biting them or buzzing too near them.)

- **Page 9** *Why do you think the people feel brave?* (The cave is deep and dark, but they are all together and look in anyway.)

- **Page 11** *What does the family see near the cave?* (They see a bat and some animal tracks.)

- **Pages 14–15** *Why does the family run away?* (They see a skunk and probably do not want to get sprayed with its bad smell.)

Reading Strategies

If... a child skips words or plural endings while reading,	**Then...** encourage the child to use his or her finger to track words and word endings.
If... a child reads unfamiliar words correctly,	**Then...** praise him or her for good word solving and checking skills.
If... a child cannot recognize cause-and-effect relationships,	**Then...** use **Model Your Thinking** below.

Model Your Thinking

Comprehension Skill: Cause and Effect

When I read, I think about what happens in a story and why it happens. For example, in this story, I wonder what happened to make the family turn and run near the end. They see some animal tracks, so I think they turned around to find out what animal made the tracks. But then they see a skunk. I know that if a skunk is afraid or disturbed, it can spray you with a terrible smell that doesn't come out of your clothes and is hard to wash off. They did not want to have the skunk spray its smell on them, so that is why they ran.

After Reading

Revisiting the Text

Comprehension Have children reread the book as a group. Encourage them to talk about what happened to the family and the cause of each of these events. Record children's thoughts in the T-Chart on page 140, using as heads the questions: *What happens?* and *Why does it happen?* Then have children use the charts to draw pictures and write captions about a favorite story event.

22B

How Bill Found Rain

by Susan McCloskey
Leveled Reader 22B
Genre: Tall Tale
Level: Easy/Average

Summary

Mom, Dad, and Sis all agree that it is just too hot and sunny. Bill collects pieces of rope from everyone and rides off to look for rain. Finally he finds a big black cloud. He ropes the cloud and brings it home, where it finally begins to rain.

Leveled Reader Practice

After children have read *How Bill Found Rain,* use Leveled Reader practice page 184 to assess their understanding of the Leveled Reader and the target comprehension skill. Additional after reading activities are provided on page 97.

At a Glance

Links to the Student Edition

⌖ **Comprehension Skill:** Cause and Effect

Selection Vocabulary: *first, been, found*

Program Theme: Journeys in Time and Space
Unit Theme: Take Me There

A young boy travels far and wide to find rain to bring back to his family's dry farmland.

Before Reading

Motivating the Reader
Build Background About the Weather

Ask children to imagine what it would be like if it was sunny and hot every day for a long time. Ask how people and animals would feel and what would happen to plants, trees, and crops. When children mention that rain would be needed, ask them about rain. Have children talk about rain and thunderstorms and share their experiences with rainy weather.

Preview and Predict

Have children scan the cover, text, and illustrations. Encourage them to use picture clues and familiar words to predict what the story is about. Prepare children for reading by saying:

> The people in this book have a problem. Read to find out what the problem is, and what the boy, Bill, does about it.

Point out selection vocabulary and any unfamiliar words that are important to understanding the book, such as *rain, rode, cloud, home,* and *kiss.*

During Reading

Guiding Comprehension

Use the following questions to support children as they read.

- **Pages 2–3** What problem does the family have? How do you know? (It has been too hot and dry. The family says they need rain. The father shows a pail full of dust. The girl uses an umbrella to protect herself from the sun. She looks at wilted plants.)

- **Page 4** What does the family need to solve their problem? (They need rain.)

- **Pages 5–7** Why does the family get rope? (Bill said he would find rain, and he asked for rope.) What do you think Bill will do with all the rope? (Predictions will vary.)

- **Pages 8–9** What is Bill looking for? (Bill is looking for a cloud.) Why does Bill want to find a big, black cloud? (Big, black clouds usually come before a rainstorm.) What will Bill do next? (He will use the rope to catch the cloud and bring it back to the family's farm.)

- **Pages 10–13** What does Bill do with the cloud? (Bill throws his rope at the cloud and tries to lasso it. Then he pulls the cloud all the way home.)

- **Page 15** What does Bill do when he gets home? (Bill pulls hard on the rope and then it begins to rain.)

- **Page 16** What things could really happen in this story? (The weather could stay hot and sunny for a long time and cause problems for the family.) What things could not really happen? (A little boy could not catch a rain cloud with rope, bring it home, and make it rain.)

Reading Strategies

If... a child stumbles over the word *sunny*,	Then... guide the child to break the word into two smaller parts.
If... a child seems confused by *pulled* and *tugged*,	Then... ask the child what familiar word he or she sees in each one. Guide the child to understand that the suffix *-ed* means the action occurred in the past.
If... a child cannot recognize cause-and-effect relationships,	Then... use **Model Your Thinking** below.

Model Your Thinking

 Comprehension Skill: Cause and Effect

Think ALOUD

As I read, I think about what happens in a story and why it happens. One thing that happens in this story is that Bill uses rope to catch a rain cloud and bring it to his family's farm. I ask myself: "Why does he do this?" I think the answer is at the beginning of the story. It is hot and dry, and it is very sunny. The family members say they need rain. That is why Bill went out to find a rain cloud.

After Reading

Revisiting the Text

Comprehension Have children take turns using the book's pictures to retell the story. A child should point to the picture and explain what is happening and why. Then have children extend the story by drawing pictures and writing words to show what effects the rain will have on the farm.

23A
Pandas

by Kimberlee Mason
Leveled Reader 23A
Genre: Informational Article
Level: Easy

Summary

This book shows pandas engaging in some of their favorite activities, such as climbing, playing, eating, and sleeping.

Leveled Reader Practice

After children have read *Pandas,* use Leveled Reader practice page 185 to assess their understanding of the Leveled Reader and the target comprehension skill. Additional after reading activities are provided on page 99.

At a Glance

Links to the Student Edition

☞ **Comprehension Skill:** Main Idea

Selection Vocabulary: *animals, their*

Program Theme: Journeys in Time and Space
Unit Theme: Take Me There

Take a journey to the mountains of China to learn about panda bears.

Before Reading

Motivating the Reader
Build Background About Pandas

Show a picture of a panda, and ask children what they know about pandas. Write their ideas in the first column of a large K-W-L chart like the one on page 133. Then ask children what they would like to learn about pandas. Write children's questions in the second column of the chart. Keep the chart on display while children read the book. After reading, have a discussion in which children tell what they learned about pandas. Enter that information in the last column of the chart.

Preview and Predict

Have children scan the cover, text, and photographs. Encourage them to use picture clues and familiar words to predict what the story is about. Prepare children for reading by saying:

> **What kind of animal is this? What do you think pandas like to do?**

Review the questions listed in the K-W-L chart. Suggest children read to look for answers to their questions and other interesting facts about pandas.

Point out selection vocabulary and any unfamiliar words that are important to understanding the book, such as *fur, habits, hide, swim, sit, roll,* and *creep.*

During Reading

● Guiding Comprehension

Use the following questions to support children as they read.

- **Page 2** Who is telling about pandas? (a girl named Su-Lin) Is Su-Lin telling about something real or make-believe? How do you know? (She is telling about something real. She gives facts about pandas, which are real animals.)

- **Pages 2–3** Where do Su-Lin and pandas live? (They both live in China.)

- **Page 3** What colors does a panda's fur have? (A panda's fur is black and white.)

- **Pages 5–6** What do you think a habit is? (Accept all reasonable responses, but guide children to read on, using the example on page 6 to figure out that a habit is a behavior that a person or animal does repeatedly.)

- **Pages 6–11** What do pandas like to do? (Pandas like to climb, hide, swim, slide, sit, and play.)

- **Pages 12–13** Do you think pandas eat a lot? Why or why not? (Yes. They eat a lot because it says they eat night and day. They are big animals, so they need a lot of food.)

- **Page 14** Do you think pandas like to have fun? Why or why not? (Yes. Rolling down a hill is fun. Earlier it said they like to swim, slide, and play—all fun activities.)

- **Page 15** Look at the picture. What do you think *creep* means? (It means "to crawl forward, low to the ground.")

- **Page 16** What do you learn about pandas on this page? (Pandas like to sleep.)

Reading Strategies

If... a child recognizes that some pages have words that rhyme and uses that to figure out some words,	**Then...** praise the child for finding helpful clues when reading.
If... a child appears to rely too heavily on the pictures to help them figure out unfamiliar words,	**Then...** point out that on pages 7 and 9, the pictures confirm a word, but they do not clearly tell what the word should be.
If... a child has difficulty identifying the book's main idea,	**Then...** use **Model Your Thinking** below.

Model Your Thinking

 Comprehension Skill: Main Idea

 Think ALOUD

Before I begin reading, I look at the words and pictures to try to figure out what the book is all about. All the pictures show a panda doing something different. Most of the sentences are about what pandas do—swim, eat, roll, sleep. So I know the book is all about what pandas like to do.

After Reading

Revisiting the Text

Comprehension Give students three choices of a main idea. Give them one correct choice and two choices of supporting details. Have children choose the main idea from these choices. Then have them tell what they learned about pandas from reading the book. Record their responses in the last column of the K-W-L chart they began before reading the book. Groups can use the chart to help them create fact file cards.

23B
What Lilly Pup Heard

by Judy Nayer
Leveled Reader 23B
Genre: Animal Fantasy
Level: Easy/Average

Summary

Lilly Pup can't read because everyone at home is making noise. So she finds a quiet spot to read and soon falls asleep. Then she hears a different noise—her family is looking for her! Last and best of all, Lilly Pup hears her mother reading to her as she falls asleep in bed.

Leveled Reader Practice

After children have read *What Lilly Pup Heard,* use Leveled Reader practice page 186 to assess their understanding of the Leveled Reader and the target comprehension skill. Additional after reading activities are provided on page 101.

At a Glance

Links to the Student Edition

Comprehension Skill: Main Idea

Selection Vocabulary: *most, even, heard*

Program Theme: Journeys in Time and Space
Unit Theme: Take Me There

You don't have to travel far from home to go on a journey, and sometimes the best part of a journey is coming home.

Before Reading

Motivating the Reader
Build Background About Favorite Activities

Tell children that the character in this book really loves to read. Ask children to think of activities they especially enjoy and have individuals pantomime doing the activity or give word clues about it for the group to guess. Then discuss the fact that sometimes it's hard to do what you enjoy, and ask if anyone has experienced that problem.

Preview and Predict

Have children scan the cover, text, and illustrations. Encourage them to use picture clues and familiar words to predict what the story is about. Draw their attention to the book title and ask:

> Whom is the book all about? What is Lilly Pup doing? What problem do you think she has?

Suggest children read to find out what problem Lilly Pup has and how she tries to solve it.

Point out selection vocabulary and any unfamiliar words that are important to understanding the book, such as *started, something, read, baby, can't, quiet,* and *told.*

During Reading

Guiding Comprehension

Use the following questions to support children as they read.

- **Pages 2–3** Why can't Lilly Pup read on her bed? (The baby is making noise, so it is hard to read.)

- **Page 3** Point to the word *can't.* **What is this word?** (can't) **What does it mean?** (It means "cannot, not able to do something.")

- **Pages 4–5** Why can't Lilly Pup read in the kitchen? (Her father is making noise with a blender.)

- **Pages 6–7** Why can't Lilly Pup read outside? (Her mother is cutting the hedges.)

- **Page 7** How do you think Lilly Pup is feeling? How do you know? (She is feeling upset and frustrated because she can't find a quiet place to read. I see an exclamation mark after her words. I know I would be upset if there was something I wanted to do, but couldn't.)

- **Pages 8–9** What is Lilly Pup's problem? (She loves her family, but she also likes to read. She can't read because everyone at home is making noise.)

- **Pages 10–11** What does Lilly Pup do to try to solve her problem? (She walks in the woods to find a quiet spot to read.) **What happens next?** (She falls asleep after reading most of her book.)

- **Pages 12–13** Why does Lilly Pup wake up? (Lilly Pup hears her family calling her. They are looking for her.)

- **Page 16** Why do you think Lilly Pup likes to hear her mother read? (She likes hearing stories. She probably likes hearing her mother's voice, and she feels loved and cared for.)

- **Page 16** What is this book all about? (It is about a young pup who is having trouble finding a quiet place to read.)

Reading Strategies

If... a child hesitates at *started*, *walked*, or *liked*,	Then... cover the *-ed*, and ask the child to read the base word. Then have the child read the whole word.
If... a child uses picture clues to explain why Lilly Pup can't read at home,	Then... praise him or her for paying attention to pictures as well as words.
If... a child has difficulty identifying the book's main idea,	Then... use **Model Your Thinking** below.

Model Your Thinking

Comprehension Skill: Main Idea

As I read, I think about what the book is all about. I look at the sentences to see how they are alike. Most of them are about Lilly Pup trying to read, but she can't because of the noise. This book is all about a young pup who likes to read, but has trouble finding a quiet place to read.

After Reading

Revisiting the Text

Comprehension Give children three choices for a main idea, with only one correct choice. Have children select the main idea from one of the three choices and draw a picture to show the main idea. Invite children to share their pictures and explain them.

24A
Why Little Possum's Tail Is Bare

by Cheyenne Cisco
Leveled Reader 24A
Genre: Fable
Level: Easy

Summary

Little Possum is a very curious animal. Even though his mother warns him about getting into trouble, his curiosity gets the best of him. But Little Possum learns an important lesson when he goes to investigate a fire up close. A spark ignites the fur on his tail, and that is why possums have bare tails to this day.

Leveled Reader Practice

After children have read *Why Little Possum's Tail Is Bare,* use Leveled Reader practice page 187 to assess their understanding of the Leveled Reader and the target comprehension skill. Additional after reading activities are provided on page 103.

At a Glance

Links to the Student Edition

⌖ **Comprehension Skill:** Cause and Effect

Selection Vocabulary: *burns, better, because*

**Program Theme: Journeys in Time and Space
Unit Theme: Take Me There**

Fables can tell stories about long ago that help us understand something about today's world, such as why possums have bare tails.

Before Reading

Motivating the Reader
Build Background About Safety Rules

Ask children to name dangers they have been warned about and what their parents, teachers, or others have said about them. Children may mention safety rules about traffic, electrical sockets and appliances, stairs, animals, matches, and fire. Have children dictate to you statements of things you should or shouldn't do in order to stay safe.

Preview and Predict

Have children scan the cover, text, and illustrations. Encourage them to use picture clues and familiar words to predict what the story is about. Prepare children for reading by saying:

> **What things does Little Possum see? What do you think his mother says about these things? What does Little Possum do?**

Explain that this story is a fable and that most fables teach a lesson. Suggest children read to find out what lesson Little Possum learns.

Point out selection vocabulary and any unfamiliar words that are important to understanding the book, such as *sting, those, light, glow, tail,* and *bare.*

During Reading

Guiding Comprehension

Use the following questions to support children as they read.

- **Pages 2–3** *What does Little Possum hear?* (He hears the buzz of a bee.) *What does Little Possum's mother tell him? What do you think she wants Little Possum to do?* (His mother tells him that bees sting. She wants him to stay away from them.)

- **Pages 4–5** *What does Little Possum do? Why do you think he does this?* (He peeks into the beehive because he is very curious.)

- **Page 5** *What do you think will happen next?* (Little Possum will get stung by a bee.)

- **Page 6** *What happened to Little Possum? Why did it happen?* (When he stuck his nose in the beehive, he got stung by a bee.)

- **Page 7** *What is Little Possum curious about now?* (a cat)

- **Page 8** *What does his mother tell him? Why does she tell him this?* (She tells him that cats bite. She wants him to stay away from the cat.)

- **Page 9** *What do you think will happen next?* (Little Possum will go close to the cat. The cat will bite or scratch him.)

- **Page 12** *What is Little Possum interested in now?* (He is curious about a fire.) *What does Mama Possum say?* (Mama Possum tells him that fire burns.)

- **Page 13** *What do you think will happen next? Why?* (Little Possum will investigate because he is too curious to listen to his mother. He will probably get hurt.)

- **Pages 14–15** *What happens to Little Possum?* (Little Possum didn't listen to his mother and went near the fire. A spark from the fire hit his tail.)

- **Page 16** *What do you think the lesson of this story is?* (The lesson is that we should always listen to our mothers.)

Reading Strategies

If...	Then...
If... a child reads very slowly,	**Then...** have him or her reread the page to become familiar with the text. Then model fluent reading and have the child read the page again, following your model.
If... a child begins to pick up the rhythm of the verses,	**Then...** praise him or her for reading fluently and observing the rhythm of the text.
If... a child cannot recognize cause-and-effect relationships,	**Then...** use **Model Your Thinking** below.

Model Your Thinking

Think ALOUD

🎯 **Comprehension Skill: Cause and Effect**

As I read, I think about what happens in the story and why it happens. On page 6, I see Mama Possum hugging Little Possum. I ask myself: "What happened?" I read and find out that he got stung by a bee. Then I ask myself: "Why did this happen?" I look back at pages 4 and 5 and see Little Possum sticking his nose in a beehive with bees all around. I know bees will sting if you get too close to them. That is why Little Possum got stung.

After Reading

Revisiting the Text

Comprehension Have pairs reread the story to find out what happens and why. Use the T-Chart on page 140 and label the columns *What happens?* and *Why?* Have children write words and/or draw pictures to show what happens to Little Possum and why it happens. Pairs can then use their charts and take turns retelling the story to one another.

24B
Many Little Beads

by Anne Sibley O'Brien
Leveled Reader 24B
Genre: Realistic Story
Level: Easy/Average

Summary

A young American girl named Robin receives a bracelet. The book traces the story of this bracelet—from the girl in Africa who makes the bracelet from many little colored beads to Robin's aunt who buys the bracelet to send to Robin. The story ends as Robin imagines going to Africa to meet the girl who made the bracelet.

Leveled Reader Practice

After children have read *Many Little Beads,* use Leveled Reader practice page 188 to assess their understanding of the Leveled Reader and the target comprehension skill. Additional after reading activities are provided on page 105.

At a Glance

Links to the Student Edition

Comprehension Skill: Cause and Effect

Selection Vocabulary: *people, put, give*

Program Theme: Journeys in Time and Space
Unit Theme: Take Me There

Even something as small as a bracelet can be part of a story about an amazing journey.

Before Reading

Motivating the Reader
Build Background About Gifts

Ask children if they have ever received gifts from a relative or friend from far away. You may wish to use a globe or world map to locate places from which children's gifts have come. Have volunteers act out someone making a gift to be sold, a person buying that gift and sending it to a friend or family member who lives far away, and that person opening the gift. Discuss why people make, buy, and give gifts, and how it feels to give or get a gift.

Preview and Predict

Have children scan the cover, text, and illustrations. Encourage them to use picture clues and familiar words to predict what the story is about. Prepare children for reading by saying:

> What do you think this book is about? Where do you think the bracelet was made? Look for the answer as you read.

Point out selection vocabulary and any unfamiliar words that are important to understanding the book, such as *woman, lady, sent, mail,* and *note.*

During Reading

Guiding Comprehension

Use the following questions to support children as they read.

- **Pages 2–3** *What do you think you will find out in this book?* (Possible answer: I'll find out how the bracelet got from the faraway girl to Robin.)

- **Page 4** *How did the girl make a bracelet?* (She put the colored beads on a string.)

- **Page 5** *Why do you think the girl and the woman have so many baskets, bracelets, and necklaces?* (They are selling them.)

- **Page 5** *Which words keep getting repeated?* ("Many little beads" and "white, yellow, blue, red, black" keep getting repeated.)

- **Pages 6–7** *What does the woman in blue do?* (She sees the bracelet, buys it, and takes a picture of the girl who made it.) *Why does the woman buy the bracelet?* (She likes the many little beads. She may want a gift for herself or someone else.)

- **Pages 8–9** *What does the woman do with the bracelet?* (She puts the bracelet in a box and sends it back home.)

- **Pages 10–11** *How is the woman who sent the bracelet related to Robin? How do you know?* (It is her aunt. Robin's mother tells her that her sister sent it.)

- **Page 14** *How do you think Robin feels about the bracelet? How do you know?* (She likes it. She puts it on. She smiles when she looks at it. I know I like getting pretty things as gifts.)

- **Page 16** *What does the bracelet cause Robin to think about?* (Robin thinks about the girl who made the bracelet, and she wonders if she will meet her one day.)

Reading Strategies

If... a child is confused by the changes of place,	**Then...** discuss where each part of the story happens. Help the child to use the pictures as clues to the transitions in setting.
If... a child has difficulty with the words *patted* and *crossed* on pages 8–9,	**Then...** cover the inflected ending in each case and have the child read the base word. Then have the child read the whole word and tell what he or she knows about words that end in *-ed*.
If... a child cannot recognize cause-and-effect relationships,	**Then...** use **Model Your Thinking** below.

Model Your Thinking

 Comprehension Skill: Cause and Effect

Think ALOUD

As I read this book, I think about what happens and why it happens. One thing that happens is that a woman sees a bracelet with many little beads. She buys it because she likes the beads, and she wants to send a gift to her niece Robin. These are reasons why she buys the bracelet.

After Reading

Revisiting the Text

Comprehension Have children take turns reading the book aloud. As they read, have them pause at natural breaking points in the story to talk about what has happened and why it happened. Give children partial sentences to complete, such as: "The woman buys a bracelet because. . . ." When they have finished the book, work together to write a thank you letter from Robin to her aunt.

25A
Wish Faces
Face Painting Fun

by Ada Evelyn
Leveled Reader 25A
Genre: How-To Article
Level: Easy

Summary

This book is a fun-filled guide to face painting. Children learn how to become a bat, a cat, a bunny—anything they can imagine!

Leveled Reader Practice

After children have read *Wish Faces,* use Leveled Reader practice page 189 to assess their understanding of the Leveled Reader and the target comprehension skill. Additional after reading activities are provided on page 107.

At a Glance

Links to the Student Edition

↪ **Comprehension Skill:** Sequence

Selection Vocabulary: *shall, wish, ground*

Program Theme: Creativity
Unit Theme: Surprise Me!

Use your creativity to express yourself!

Before Reading

Motivating the Reader
Build Background About Face Painting

Ask children if they have ever had their faces painted. Encourage them to share their experiences with the class. Have children tell where they had their faces painted, such as at a fair, and what they had painted on their faces. Have children draw pictures of their own faces painted to look like someone or something else.

Preview and Predict

Have children scan the cover, text, and illustrations. Encourage them to use picture clues and familiar words to predict what the story is about. Prepare children for reading by saying:

> What do you think you will find out from reading this book? As you read, pay careful attention to the steps in the instructions near the end of the book.

Have children set their own purpose for reading, such as reading to find out how to make a wish face of a particular animal.

Point out selection vocabulary and any unfamiliar words that are important to understanding the book, such as *brush, watercolor,* and *paint.*

During Reading

● Guiding Comprehension

Use the following questions to support children as they read.

- **Pages 2–3** *What do you think you will learn about? How do you know?* (I will be learning about something that involves painting. I see paints, a brush, and drawings and pictures on the table.)

- **Page 4** *What has happened to the boy?* (The woman painted a bat on the boy's face.)

- **Page 5** *What does the boy wish to be now?* (a cat)

- **Page 5** *What do you think you will see on the next page?* (The boy will have his face painted to look like a cat.)

- **Pages 8–11** *What other ways do we see the boy with his face painted?* (We see the boy as a rabbit, a clown, and a zebra.)

- **Pages 14–15** *What do you have to do first?* (You have to get a brush, water, and watercolor paint.) *What do you have to do next?* (Next you have to draw what you want to be.) *What is the last step?* (You paint on your face or someone else's face.)

- **Page 16** *What would you wish to be?* (Encourage well-supported answers.)

Ongoing Assessment

Reading Strategies

If...	Then...
If... a child misreads words because he or she is reading too quickly,	**Then...** have him or her read more slowly, following the words with a fingertip.
If... a child reads rhythmically, pausing at the ends of sentences and groups of sentences,	**Then...** praise him or her for reading fluently and recognizing rhymes and rhythm.
If... a child has difficulty following the sequence of events,	**Then...** use **Model Your Thinking** below.

Model Your Thinking

 Comprehension Skill: Sequence

When I read a book that teaches me how to do something, I have to pay careful attention to the order of the steps in the instructions. Clue words such as *first, next,* and *then* can help me figure out the order. How do I paint a wish face? First, I have to get the things I need. Next, I draw the face I want. Then, I paint!

After Reading

Revisiting the Text

Comprehension Have children reread the book with a partner and use the Sequence Chart on page 139 to draw or write the steps for face painting. At the top, write a title: *How to Paint a Wish Face.* Partners can then use their charts to make wish faces like those in the book or something of their own design.

25B

The Toymaker

by Amy Hutchings
Leveled Reader 25B
Genre: Informational Article
Level: Easy/Average

Summary

This book introduces readers to a toymaker and follows the making of a new toy from the planning stages to the finished product.

Leveled Reader Practice

After children have read *The Toymaker,* use Leveled Reader practice page 190 to assess their understanding of the Leveled Reader and the target comprehension skill. Additional after reading activities are provided on page 109.

At a Glance

Links to the Student Edition

📌 **Comprehension Skill:** Sequence

Selection Vocabulary: *much, these, work*

Program Theme: Creativity
Unit Theme: Surprise Me!

Toymakers use their creativity to make toys that are lots of fun!

Before Reading

Motivating the Reader
Build Background About Toys

Display three or four toys made from different materials, and then ask children what they think each is made of. Then ask children how they think each toy was made. Discuss the work that toymakers do and whether making toys would be a fun and interesting job. Tell them that they will be reading about a man who creates toys.

Preview and Predict

Have children scan the cover, text, and illustrations. Encourage them to use picture clues and familiar words to predict what the story is about. Prepare children for reading by saying:

> What kinds of things do you think you will see in a toymaker's shop? What do you think is the very first thing the toymaker needs to do to make a new toy?

Have children use these questions to set their own purpose for reading, such as reading to find out what toy the toymaker is making.

Point out selection vocabulary and any unfamiliar words that are important to understanding the book, such as *shapes, saw, sands, sandpaper, glue, workshop, spin,* and *finished.*

During Reading

Guiding Comprehension

Use the following questions to support children as they read.

- **Page 2** What does Bill do? (He makes toys.)

- **Page 3** What do you think is the very first step in making a toy? (First you have to come up with an idea of what to make.)

- **Pages 4–5** What two steps does the toymaker take next? (He draws a plan of the new toy. Then he collects materials he will need.)

- **Page 5** What do you think Bill will do with the rulers and buttons? Why? (He will use them to make the airplane. His drawing shows two wheels that look like buttons. The sides of the plane have almost the same shape as the rulers.)

- **Page 7** Now what does the toymaker do? What material is he working with? What tool does he use? (He cuts out the shapes from wood, using a saw.)

- **Pages 8–9** Why do you think Bill sands the wood? (He sands the wood to make it smooth.) What is the glue for? (The glue holds the parts together.)

- **Pages 10–11** What happens after all the parts are glued together? (Bill paints them.)

- **Page 12** What does Bill do last? (Bill cleans up his workshop while he waits for the paint to dry.)

- **Page 13** What were the buttons and rulers for? (The buttons were used as wheels on the airplane. The rulers were used for the body of the airplane.)

- **Page 15** What word means almost the same as finished? (done, complete)

- **Page 16** Why do you think Bill is a toymaker? (Possible answers: He likes the work. It is fun.)

Reading Strategies

If...	Then...
If... a child has difficulty with the words *sandpaper* and *workshop*,	**Then...** suggest that he or she look for the two smaller words in each big word, and decode them.
If... a child seems overwhelmed by new words,	**Then...** encourage him or her to read on to the end of a sentence and predict a new word, using letter-sound knowledge. Then the child can check the meaning using picture clues and context.
If... a child has difficulty following the sequence of events,	**Then...** use **Model Your Thinking** below.

Model Your Thinking

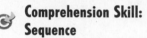

Comprehension Skill: Sequence

Think ALOUD

This book tells all about how a toymaker makes a toy airplane. As I read, I try to follow the order of the steps in making a toy. Clue words like *first, next,* and *then* help me figure out the order of what Bill does. First Bill plans his toy. He makes a drawing of all the parts. Then he collects the things he will need, like the buttons and rulers. Now he can start to make the toy. First he cuts the wood with a saw to make different shapes. If I continue to read page by page, I will find out the rest of the steps Bill does to make the toy.

After Reading

Revisiting the Text

Comprehension Create a large class flowchart. Have volunteers reread the book aloud. Have them pause after each new step is introduced and tell what the step is. Write it in the flowchart. Then ask children questions to strengthen their knowledge of the sequence of steps in making a toy, such as: "What step comes after collecting the materials?"

26A
Look at Him Go!

by Susan McCloskey
Leveled Reader 26A
Genre: Fantasy
Level: Easy

Summary

Luke is a big truck full of bikes. He can travel in hot weather and cold weather, up hills and down hills. But one day Luke gets stuck on a very steep hill. The driver asks children in the neighborhood to help by riding the bikes up the hill. It works, and Luke is able to continue on his way!

Leveled Reader Practice

After children have read *Look at Him Go!,* use Leveled Reader practice page 191 to assess their understanding of the Leveled Reader and the target comprehension skill. Additional after reading activities are provided on page 111.

At a Glance

Links to the Student Edition

⟳ **Comprehension Skill:** Theme

Selection Vocabulary: *full, cold, would*

Program Theme: Creativity
Unit Theme: Surprise Me!

Sometimes, a difficult problem calls for a creative solution. By working together and helping one another, we can solve problems.

Before Reading

Motivating the Reader
Build Background About Trucks

Ask children what kinds of trucks they have seen, and write the items on the chalkboard. Elicit from children a variety of kinds of trucks, such as a dump truck, a pickup truck, a cement truck, a moving truck, and so on. Discuss with children how people know how much to put in each truck and what might happen if a truck tries to carry too big of a load. By thinking about these issues, children will more readily identify the problem Luke and his driver face.

Preview and Predict

Have children scan the cover, text, and illustrations. Encourage them to use picture clues and familiar words to predict what the story is about. Draw their attention to the first two pages, and Luke's face. Make sure children understand that Luke is the truck. Prepare children for reading by asking:

> Who is Luke? What is Luke carrying? Read to find out what problem Luke and his driver have, and how they solve it.

Point out selection vocabulary and any unfamiliar words that are important to understanding the book, such as *lots, hard,* and *sometimes.*

During Reading

Guiding Comprehension

Use the following questions to support children as they read.

- **Pages 2–3** **Who is Luke?** (He is the yellow truck.) **What is Luke carrying?** (Luke is carrying lots and lots of bikes.)

- **Pages 4–7** **How would you describe Luke in your own words?** (Luke is a strong and dependable truck. He works hard and likes his job. He can travel in any kind of weather and over any kind of land.)

- **Pages 4–7** **What kinds of places does Luke go?** (He goes to hot and cold places. He goes up and down hills.)

- **Page 10** **What has happened to Luke? Why?** (He is stuck on a hill that is too big for him to get up. He is too full of bikes.)

- **Page 11** **How do you think this problem will be solved?** (Maybe people will ride the bikes up the hill so that Luke won't have to carry so many.)

- **Pages 12–15** **Was your prediction right? What happened?** (Yes. Luke was able to go to the top because his load was less heavy.)

- **Page 15** **How do Luke and his driver feel?** (They are glad and thankful for the help the children gave.)

- **Page 16** **What is the big idea of this book? What did you learn about helping?** (We all need help sometimes. If we all help, we can solve problems.)

Ongoing Assessment

Reading Strategies

If... a child hesitates when reading but says the right word,	**Then...** ask him or her what he or she noticed that helped him or her know the word.
If... a child makes good story predictions,	**Then...** praise him or her for using prior knowledge and clues on the page to predict.
If... a child has difficulty determining the theme,	**Then...** use **Model Your Thinking** below.

Model Your Thinking

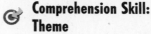

Comprehension Skill: Theme

Every story has a theme, or a big idea, that teaches us something. As I read, I think about what the story is all about and what lessons I can learn from reading it. This book is about a very strong truck named Luke. But when Luke gets stuck on a big hill, the driver says something important: "We all need help sometimes." The driver asks people to make Luke's load lighter by riding some of the bikes up the hill. She says, "Let's all help. We can do it together." That's important too. So I think the theme is that we all need help sometimes, and that when we ask for or give help, we can solve a problem.

After Reading

Revisiting the Text

Comprehension Have children use the Plot-Story Sequence Chart on page 134 to identify the book's theme. Go through the book together, summarizing pages 2–7 in the first box. Then have children summarize the problem and what the driver says about it. Finally, have children state the message of pages 12–16 in the third box.

26B
The Three Hares

A Folk Tale from Turkey

by Kana Riley
Leveled Reader 26B
Genre: Play
Level: Easy/Average

Summary

Papa Hare tells his three children that they must dig deep dens to keep themselves safe. Two of the children are lazy and build houses of flowers and leaves. A fox destroys both their homes. The third child digs a deep den. The other two siblings come to her for shelter when the fox threatens them. They all learn a valuable lesson about following the wise advice of elders.

Leveled Reader Practice

After children have read *The Three Hares,* use Leveled Reader practice page 192 to assess their understanding of the Leveled Reader and the target comprehension skill. Additional after reading activities are provided on page 113.

At a Glance

Links to the Student Edition

☞ **Comprehension Skill:** Theme

Selection Vocabulary: *off, before*

Program Theme: Creativity
Unit Theme: Surprise Me!

Putting on a play is a creative way to tell a story. In this play, some lazy, young hares learn that they should have taken their papa's wise advice.

Before Reading

Motivating the Reader
Build Background About Plays

Ask children whether they have seen a play, and what happens in a play. Draw a word web on the chalkboard, and record children's ideas about the characteristics of a play in it.

Preview and Predict

Have children scan the cover, text, and illustrations. Encourage them to use picture clues and familiar words to predict what the play is about. Prepare children for reading by saying:

> Who are the characters in this play? How can you tell which character is speaking? Look at the colors of the rabbit ears the children wear and the color behind the rabbit faces near the words.

Suggest children read to find out what happens to the three hares and what lesson they learn.

Point out selection vocabulary and any unfamiliar words that are important to understanding the book, such as *grown, digging, safe, pretty,* and *shovel.*

During Reading

Guiding Comprehension

Use the following questions to support children as they read.

- **Page 2** *How do you know who is speaking each line?* (There are little pictures of hares in different colored circles. And each hare in the photo is wearing a pair of rabbit ears in a different color that matches the pictures below.)

- **Page 3** *Why do you think the father tells the young hares to dig deep dens?* (He wants to make sure they are safe now that they are going off to live on their own.)

- **Pages 4–7** *What happens to the first hare?* (The first hare doesn't do what her father tells her. She builds a house made of flowers, but a fox comes along and smashes it down. She runs away.)

- **Page 6** *What does bim, bam, and bash mean?* (*Bim* and *bam* are nonsense words for the sounds the fox makes bashing, or wrecking, the houses.)

- **Pages 8–11** *What happens to the second hare?* (The second hare also doesn't do what his father tells him. He builds a house made of leaves, but the fox comes along and smashes it down too. He runs away.)

- **Page 11** *Why didn't the first two hares listen to their father?* (They are lazy. They thought digging a hole was too much work.)

- **Pages 12–13** *What does the third hare do?* (She follows her father's advice and digs a deep den.)

- **Page 16** *What happens to the hares?* (The first two hares run to the third hare's den. They safely hide from the fox.) **What lesson have the first two hares learned?** (They learned that they should have listened to and done what their father asked them to do.) **What will the first two hares do now?** (They will borrow their sister's shovel and dig dens of their own.)

Reading Strategies

If... a child reads a difficult word incorrectly,	**Then...** ask him or her if the word looks and sounds right. Ask the child to look at the letters and think about which word would sound right.
If... a child has difficulty determining the theme,	**Then...** use **Model Your Thinking** below.

Model Your Thinking

Comprehension Skill: Theme

Think ALOUD

Every story has a theme, or a big idea, that teaches us something. As I read, I think about what the story is all about and what lesson it teaches. In this play, Papa Hare tells his children that they must *go out into the world by themselves.* He tells them to dig deep dens to keep safe. The first two hares are lazy and do not listen to their father. But when Fox bashes down both of their weak houses, they wish they had done what their father said to do. They decide they need to dig deep dens too. So I think the theme is that you should always follow your parent's advice, and do whatever work you need to do to be happy and safe, even if it is difficult.

After Reading

Revisiting the Text

Comprehension Have groups read the play aloud, each taking one or more parts. Have children discuss what the theme of the play is. Then have the groups extend the play where the hares tell their father what happened and what lessons they've learned.

27A
Which Is Which?

by Sharon Fear
Leveled Reader 27A
Genre: Animal Fantasy
Level: Easy

Summary

Mother Pig has three babies, Fay, May, and Kay, but she can't tell them apart. Then Mother Pig has an idea. She curls each piglet's tail in a different way in order to tell them apart. And that's why pigs have curly tails!

Leveled Reader Practice

After children have read *Which Is Which?*, use Leveled Reader practice page 193 to assess their understanding of the Leveled Reader and the target comprehension skill. Additional after reading activities are provided on page 115.

At a Glance

Links to the Student Edition

Comprehension Skill: Drawing Conclusions

Selection Vocabulary: *once, under, which*

Program Theme: Creativity
Unit Theme: Surprise Me!

A mother comes up with a creative way to distinguish among her children in this clever pourquois tale.

Before Reading

Motivating the Reader
Build Background About Pourquois Tales

Ask children what stories they know or have heard that explain how something in the world came to be, such as where Bat came from or why possums' tails are bare. Invite children to retell the tales and ask if each one is realistic or make believe. Have children give reasons for their thinking. Then tell children that different cultures have always created tales that explain how something came to be.

Preview and Predict

Have children scan the cover, text, and illustrations. Encourage them to use picture clues and familiar words to make a prediction of what the story is about. Prepare children for reading by saying:

> What do you think the mother pig's problem is? How do you think her children feel about it? How do you think the problem will be solved?

Suggest children read to find out if their predictions are correct.

Point out selection vocabulary and any unfamiliar words that are important to understanding the book, such as *babies, could, fence, cried, curled,* and *know.*

During Reading

● Guiding Comprehension

Use the following questions to support children as they read.

- **Page 2** *Where does this story take place? How do you know?* (It takes place on a farm. I can see pigs, a barn, and some cows in the background.)

- **Page 3** *What do these sentences below the picture tell you?* (They tell the names of the three baby pigs.)

- **Pages 4–5** *What is the problem?* (No one, not even the mother pig, can tell the three babies apart. They all look the same.)

- **Page 6** *Who does the mother pig think she is talking to?* (Fay) *Who is she really talking to?* (May)

- **Page 7** *Why does the mother pig say, "Oops!"?* (She makes a mistake. She thinks she is talking to Kay, but she is really talking to Fay.)

- **Pages 8–9** *What does Kay do?* (She goes under the fence.) *Why is this action not a good thing to do?* (Her mother has told her not to do it. She could get hurt outside the fenced-in area.)

- **Pages 10–11** *Why do you think Fay cries?* (She cries because her mother thinks she is Kay and gets mad at her.) *What is the mother pig's plan?* (She curls each baby's tail.)

- **Pages 14–15** *Does the mother pig's plan work? Why?* (Yes. She can now tell her babies apart because each one has a tail that curls in a different way.)

- **Page 16** *Why do pigs have curly tails?* (Pigs have curly tails, so their mothers will be able to tell them apart.)

Reading Strategies

If... a child stumbles at *babies* on page 2,	Then... guide him or her understand that *babies* is the plural of *baby*.
If... a child stops at a difficult word,	Then... encourage her or him to read on to the end of the sentence and predict the word.
If... a child has difficulty drawing logical conclusions,	Then... use **Model Your Thinking** below.

Model Your Thinking

 Comprehension Skill: Drawing Conclusions

Think ALOUD

Sometimes an author doesn't tell you everything about characters or what happens in a story. I can figure out more about characters and events, if I think about what I've read and what I know from real life. For example, on page 9, I can figure out that the mother pig is upset because Kay went under the fence. I see the frown on the mother pig's face. All her words have an exclamation point at the end. I also know that mothers get upset when their children disobey them. All these clues help me figure out how the mother pig is feeling.

After Reading

Revisiting the Text

Comprehension Have children reread the book and use the Problem-Solution Chart on page 137. Invite children to tell the problem Mother Pig had with her babies, and to give examples. They can write their ideas in the Problem box on the chart. Then have them talk about what Mother Pig did and write that in the Solution box. Ask children to draw a conclusion and write a sentence about why Mother Pig curled her babies' tails.

27B
How Crayons Are Made

by Phoebe Marsh
Leveled Reader 27B
Genre: Informational Article
Level: Easy/Average

Summary

This book describes how crayons are made, detailing each stage in the process from melting the wax to boxing them to be shipped to stores. The book ends with a few ways to have fun drawing with crayons.

Leveled Reader Practice

After children have read *How Crayons Are Made,* use Leveled Reader practice page 194 to assess their understanding of the Leveled Reader and the target comprehension skill. Additional after reading activities are provided on page 117.

At a Glance

Links to the Student Edition

⟳ **Comprehension Skill:** Drawing Conclusions

Selection Vocabulary: *each, other*

Program Theme: Creativity
Unit Theme: Surprise Me!

Crayons are one tool we can use to express our creativity in colorful ways.

Before Reading

Motivating the Reader
Build Background About Crayons

Help children fill out the K-W-L chart on page 133. Begin with what children know about crayons. Then invite children's questions about crayons. Children may ask, "How do they get the color in?" and "How do they get them all the same shape?" Later, after reading the book, children can write in the third column answers to the questions and other things they learned from the book.

Preview and Predict

Have children scan the cover, text, and illustrations. Encourage them to use picture clues and familiar words to predict what the story is about. Prepare children for reading by saying:

> What kind of place do you think you will read about in this book? What are people doing in this book? What do you think you will learn from reading this book?

Review the questions about crayons that children wrote in their K-W-L charts. Encourage children to use these questions to help them set a purpose for their reading.

Point out selection vocabulary and any unfamiliar words that are important to understanding the book, such as *wax, color, molds, paper, best, truck,* and *stores.*

During Reading

Guiding Comprehension

Use the following questions to support children as they read.

- **Pages 2–3** *How are crayons alike? How are they different?* (Children can use both the text and prior knowledge to answer. Alike: They are fun. They are all made the same way. Different: Some are big, and others are small. They come in different colors.)

- **Pages 4–5** *What are crayons made of?* (Crayons are made of wax.) *What happens after the wax gets hot and soft?* (The color is mixed into the wax.)

- **Pages 6–7** *What happens next?* (The wax is poured into molds.) *What happens when the wax cools off?* (When the wax cools off, it gets hard.)

- **Pages 8–9** *What happens to the crayons now?* (Paper is put around each crayon, and each color gets a name.) *What do the labels on the crayons tell?* (The labels tell what color the crayon is.)

- **Pages 10–11** *What happens now?* (The crayons are put into different-sized boxes.)

- **Pages 12–13** *How do crayons get to your house?* (Big boxes full of crayon boxes are put on trucks and then are taken to stores. I can buy some crayons at a store and take them home.)

- **Page 14** *What does it mean to "fill your hand with crayons"?* (It means to hold a bunch of crayons in your hand at once like the girl is doing in the picture.)

- **Pages 14–15** *Whare are these two pages all about?* (They tell two ways to have fun with crayons.) *What other things do you like to do with crayons?* (Accept all reasonable responses.)

Reading Strategies

If... a child is confused about what happens on pages 6–7,	**Then...** have him or her think about water hardening into ice in ice cube trays.
If... a child has trouble drawing logical conclusions,	**Then...** use **Model Your Thinking** below.

Model Your Thinking

 Comprehension Skill: Drawing Conclusions

Think ALOUD

Sometimes authors don't tell you everything about what happens in a book. For example this book tells that the crayons get wrapped and boxed. The boxes of crayons go to stores, and some go to our houses. I can figure out more about these events by thinking about what I've read, looking at picture clues, and what I already know about stores and crayons. I see that on page 11, workers put the different colors of crayons into the boxes in which we buy them. But on page 12, they are loading bigger boxes on the truck. I conclude that many little boxes are packed into bigger cardboard boxes, to make it easier to carry lots of crayons to stores. The stores must order lots of crayons and have them delivered. Then they open the big cardboard boxes and put out the crayon boxes for us to buy. The crayons get to our houses when we buy them and take them home.

After Reading

Revisiting the Text

Comprehension Have children reread the book, and complete the K-W-L charts that they began before reading. Have them tell what they learned about crayons and list it in the third column. Ask questions to help them draw conclusions about the book.

28A
Yes, But

by Kana Riley
Leveled Reader 28A
Genre: Animal Fantasy
Level: Easy

Summary

Squirrel shows off her new home to her friends. They all like it, but each one has an idea of how to make it better. Squirrel is not happy with the way they have redecorated her new home. She asks her friends to help her put her things back the way she wants them.

Leveled Reader Practice

After children have read *Yes, But,* use Leveled Reader practice page 195 to assess their understanding of the Leveled Reader and the target comprehension skill. Additional after reading activities are provided on page 119.

At a Glance

Links to the Student Edition

☞ **Comprehension Skill:** Plot

Selection Vocabulary: *great, idea, along, pull*

Program Theme: Creativity
Unit Theme: Surprise Me!

We all have our own individual ways of expressing ourselves. What looks great to one person may not look great to another.

Before Reading

Motivating the Reader
Build Background About Animals' Homes

Ask children where they think crows make their homes, and what their homes might be like. Repeat these questions for mice and spiders. Point out, if necessary, that crows have nests high in trees, that mice live between walls and under floors in tiny homes, and that spiders are usually found in webs. Then ask how children think any of these animals would feel if they had to live in a different kind of place. Guide children to understand that each animal probably likes its own kind of home best.

Preview and Predict

Have children scan the cover, text, and illustrations. Encourage them to use picture clues and familiar words to predict what the book is about. Prepare children for reading by saying:

> **What is this book about? Who are the characters? What do you think will happen? Read to find out what problem arises.**

Point out selection vocabulary and any unfamiliar words that are important to understanding the book, such as *idea, took,* and *low.* Ask children to tell what they think the book title means and where they might have heard someone say, "Yes, but . . . ."

During Reading

⬤ Guiding Comprehension

Use the following questions to support children as they read.

- **Pages 2–3** *What does Squirrel want to show her friends?* (She wants to show them her new house.) *Which of her friends comes to visit first?* (Crow comes to visit first.)

- **Pages 4–5** *Why do you think Crow puts things up high?* (Crows live high up in trees, so Crow piles things up to be like a tree.)

- **Pages 6–7** *Who comes to visit next?* (Mouse comes to visit next.) *What do you think he will do?* (He will put Squirrel's things the way he likes to have them.)

- **Page 8** *Why does Mouse pull things down low?* (Mice like to hide underneath things, so Mouse thinks the house looks great when things are pulled down low.)

- **Page 9** *Who comes to visit Squirrel next?* (Spider comes to visit next.) *What will happen next?* (Spider will say she likes the house, but then she will change things so they look the way a spider would like them.)

- **Pages 12–13** *How do you think Squirrel feels?* (Squirrel is unhappy because her things are not arranged the way she wants them to be.) *What do you think she will do?* (Maybe she will get her friends to put her things back the way she wants.)

- **Page 16** *How does the story end?* (Squirrel tells her friends to put her things back the way they found them, and then she says, "Now it looks great!")

- **Page 16** *What do you think is the big idea of this story?* (Possible answers: What looks great to one person may not look great to another. Everyone has their own way of making a home special.)

Reading Strategies

If... a child is confused by quotation marks,	**Then...** have the child tell who is speaking on each page and show how he or she knows. Then have the child reread the pages, saying the words in quotation marks in the animals' voices.
If... a child makes accurate predictions about what the animals will say and do,	**Then...** praise the child for recognizing the story pattern and using it to make predictions.
If... a child has trouble describing the plot,	**Then...** use **Model Your Thinking** below.

Model Your Thinking

 Comprehension Skill: Plot

 Think ALOUD

The plot of a story is what happens first, next, and last in the story. In this story, the first thing that happens is Squirrel wants to show off her new home to her friends. But when she shows it to her friends, each one changes it to the way he or she would like it. But Squirrel doesn't like it any of those ways. The story ends when Squirrel asks all her friends to help; she asks them to push and pull to get everything back the way she likes it.

After Reading

Revisiting the Text

Comprehension Have pairs reread the book, and use the Plot/Story Sequence Chart on page 134 to tell what happens in the beginning, middle, and end of the story. Children can write words and/or draw pictures in each box. Encourage pairs to use their charts to retell the story in their own words to another pair.

28B

Mr. Small

by Fay Robinson
Leveled Reader 28B
Genre: Humorous Story
Level: Easy/Average

Summary

Mr. Small wants to fly like a bird. He makes wings, feathers, and a beak, but still he cannot fly. Then he makes a nest in a tree. There he makes some bird friends. Mr. Small still cannot fly, but he is happy with his new friends.

Leveled Reader Practice

After children have read *Mr. Small,* use Leveled Reader practice page 196 to assess their understanding of the Leveled Reader and the target comprehension skill. Additional after reading activities are provided on page 121.

At a Glance

Links to the Student Edition

☞ **Comprehension Skill:** Plot

Selection Vocabulary: *goes, pull*

Program Theme: Creativity
Unit Theme: Surprise Me!

Mr. Small comes up with some creative ideas in his attempt to fly.

Before Reading

Motivating the Reader
Build Background About Birds

Show children pictures or videotapes of birds. Have children share what they know about birds, such as how they move, what body parts they have, and where they live. Have groups draw pictures of a bird they like and label its head, tail, wings, beak, claws, and so on.

Preview and Predict

Have children scan the cover, text, and illustrations. Encourage them to use picture clues and familiar words to predict what the book is about. Prepare children for reading by saying:

> Who is this story all about? What does Mr. Small want to do? Do you think his ideas will work? Read to find out what happens to Mr. Small.

Point out selection vocabulary and any unfamiliar words that are important to understanding the book, such as *wings, feathers, beak, nest,* and *never.*

During Reading

Guiding Comprehension

Use the following questions to support children as they read.

- **Pages 2–3** Why *does* Mr. Small *want to fly?* (He sees how high and fast a bird can fly. He thinks flying looks like fun.)

- **Pages 4–5** What *does* Mr. Small *do in order to fly? What do you think will happen? Why?* (He makes some wings. I don't think they will work because people can't fly like birds can.)

- **Pages 6–7** *Does* Mr. Small *fly?* (No, he does not fly.) What *does* Mr. Small *think will help him fly now? Do you think this will work?* (Now he makes some feathers, but I don't think that will work either.)

- **Page 9** What *do you think will happen next? Why?* (Mr. Small will look at his book about birds and try to find another way to fly. This is what he has done before. He doesn't seem like a person who gives up easily.)

- **Pages 10–14** What else *does* Mr. Small *do in order to fly?* (He makes a beak. He builds a nest.)

- **Page 15** Who is Mr. Small's friend? (the bird in the small nest) *Why do you think Mr. Small and the bird become friends?* (Mr. Small looks like a bird, so maybe the bird thinks he is a bird. Mr. Small likes birds.)

- **Page 16** How *does the story end?* (Mr. Small never learns to fly, but he makes some bird friends.) *Why do you think Mr. Small is happy even though he never did fly?* (Mr. Small is happy because he has made some friends.)

Ongoing Assessment

Reading Strategies

If... a child skips the -*ed* endings in *pulled* and *worked,*

Then... have the child reread these words, tracing the letters with a finger.

If... a child uses the sentence patterns to help in reading fluently,

Then... praise him or her for recognizing and using the patterns.

If... a child has difficulty determining the plot of the story,

Then... use **Model Your Thinking** below.

Model Your Thinking

 Comprehension Skill: Plot

The plot is what happens first, next, and last in a story. At the beginning of the story, I read that Mr. Small wants to fly. The middle of the story shows the different ways he tries to fly by making wings, feathers, a beak, and a nest. At the end, it says that Mr. Small never did get to fly. But he was happy anyway, because he had made new friends.

After Reading

Revisiting the Text

Comprehension Have pairs reread the book and use the Plot/Story Sequence Chart on page 134 to tell what happens in the beginning, middle, and end of the story. Have pairs use their charts to help them act out the story events.

29A
Almost

by Nat Gabriel
Leveled Reader 29A
Genre: Realistic Story
Level: Easy

Summary

Ted is more daring than his friend Ned when it comes to jumping into pools or swinging on a swing. But the tables are turned at the end, when Ned jumps on a seesaw and has to help a less daring Ted get on.

Leveled Reader Practice

After children have read *Almost,* use Leveled Reader practice page 197 to assess their understanding of the Leveled Reader and the target comprehension skill. Additional after reading activities are provided on page 123.

At a Glance

Links to the Student Edition

☞ **Comprehension Skill:** Theme

Selection Vocabulary: *took, almost*

Program Theme: Creativity
Unit Theme: Surprise Me!

Some problems require creative solutions, but having a friend's help makes solving them easier.

Before Reading

Motivating the Reader
Build Background About Fears

Ask children if they are sometimes afraid to do something new, and make a list of things that children say are hard or scary for them to do. Have children tell how they got over their fears, and identify some ways to help oneself take the first step. Have volunteers act out a situation where one friend helps another friend who is scared to try something new.

Preview and Predict

Have children scan the cover, text, and illustrations. Encourage them to use picture clues and familiar words to predict what the book is about. Prepare children for reading by saying:

> How are these boys alike? How are they different? Look at their faces. How do you think each boy feels? Read to find out what happens to them. Think about what the big idea, or theme, of this story is.

Point out selection vocabulary and any unfamiliar words that are important to understanding the book, such as *quite, splash, swing, apple,* and *seesaw.*

During Reading

Guiding Comprehension

Use the following questions to support children as they read.

- **Pages 2–3 What does Ted do? What does Ned do?** (Ted jumps into the pool. Ned almost jumps in, but doesn't.)

- **Pages 4–5 How do you think Ted and Ned are different?** (Ted isn't afraid to do things like jump off a diving board into a pool. Ned is scared and won't jump into pools.)

- **Page 7 Why do you think Ned decides not to jump over the gap between the two logs?** (He might be afraid he will fall and get hurt or that he won't do it right and look silly.)

- **Pages 8–9 What does Ted do?** (Ted jumps on a swing.) **What does Ned do?** (Ned looks but does not get on the swing.)

- **Pages 10–11 What happens to Ned?** (Ned doesn't get an apple like Ted, and he almost cries.)

- **Page 12 What does Ted do?** (Ted gives Ned some of his apple and tells him that that's what friends are for.) **What does this action tell you about Ted?** (He is nice. He is a good friend.)

- **Page 12 Read Ted's words. What do they mean?** (Ted means that friends share with one another.)

- **Pages 14–15 Why doesn't Ted get right on the seesaw? How does Ned help him?** (The end of the seesaw is too high for Ted to get on. Ned stands up and picks up his end of the seesaw, so the other end won't be so high. Now Ted can get on.)

- **Page 16 How do both boys feel now? Why?** (They are both happy because they've helped each other.)

- **Page 16 What is the big idea, or theme, of this story?** (Possible answers: Friends help one another. Friends can make you feel better.)

Ongoing Assessment

Reading Strategies

If... a child hesitates when reading but then says the correct word,

Then... ask him or her what he or she noticed that helped him or her know that word.

If... a child reads too slowly, pausing frequently,

Then... model fluent reading for him or her. Remind the child that reading can sound just like talking. Have the child reread the page, following your model.

If... a child has trouble identifying the theme,

Then... use **Model Your Thinking** below.

Model Your Thinking

 Comprehension Skill: Theme

Think ALOUD

Every story has a big idea, or theme. As I read, I think about the story's big idea, or theme. I ask myself: "What have the characters learned? What can I learn from reading this story?" At first, Ted and Ned seem very different. Ted is daring and likes to try new things. Ned would like to do these things too, but he is afraid. But when Ted shares his apple with Ned, I see the two boys are friends. Next, it is Ned who helps Ted get on the seesaw. Both boys say the same thing. "That is what friends are for!" I think the theme of this story is that friends help one another. That is something important we all can learn about being a good friend.

After Reading

Revisiting the Text

Comprehension Have children reread the book and use the T-Chart on page 140 to list details about Ted and Ned. Encourage children to think about what lesson these characters have learned. Have them write a sentence and draw a picture about the story's big idea, or theme.

29B
Panda Picture

by Louisa Ernesto
Leveled Reader 29B
Genre: Fantasy
Level: Easy/Average

Summary

A girl thinks she sees a panda on a bus, at the library, at a hair salon, on a boat, and on a statue in the park. She finally takes a picture to prove that it's real. Then she finds out that a zoo really lost a panda. She has a picture to prove something else as well. They lost a zebra too!

Leveled Reader Practice

After children have read *Panda Picture,* use Leveled Reader practice page 198 to assess their understanding of the Leveled Reader and the target comprehension skill. Additional after reading activities are provided on page 125.

At a Glance

Links to the Student Edition

⌖ **Comprehension Skill:** Theme

Selection Vocabulary: *knew, thought, picture*

Program Theme: Creativity
Unit Theme: Surprise Me!

Sometimes, we see things that surprise our eyes.

Before Reading

Motivating the Reader
Build Background About Pandas

Invite children to share what they know about pandas, including what they look like, what they eat, and what they do. Then have them pretend that they have taken a photograph of a panda doing something funny, in a place where you would not normally see a panda. Have them draw their "snapshot" of a panda on art paper with crayons or markers. Then have them display their panda pictures for all to see.

Preview and Predict

Have children scan the cover, text, and illustrations. Encourage them to use picture clues and familiar words to predict what the book is about. Prepare children for reading by saying:

> What does the girl keep seeing? Are these places where you normally see a panda? Read to find out what the girl does about what she sees—and what else she finds out.

Point out selection vocabulary and any unfamiliar words that are important to understanding the book, such as *couldn't, really, sail,* and *zebra.*

During Reading

Guiding Comprehension

Use the following questions to support children as they read.

- **Pages 2–3** **What is the girl doing?** (She is getting ready to take a picture.) **What does she see?** (The girl sees a panda looking back at her.)

- **Pages 4–5** **Where does the girl think she sees a panda now?** (She thinks she sees a panda on a bus.) **Why doesn't the girl believe what she sees?** (She knows pandas don't ride buses, so she can't believe she really saw a panda.) **What two words rhyme on these pages?** (*be* and *see*)

- **Pages 6–7** **Where does the girl think she sees a panda?** (The girl thinks she sees a panda at the library sitting in a chair and reading a book.)

- **Pages 8–9** **Where does the girl see the panda next? How do you know?** (She thinks she sees a panda in a beauty shop. I see a chair like they use in a beauty shop, and a beauty shop is a place where you can get your hair curled.)

- **Pages 10–11** **How would you feel if you saw a panda sailing a boat? Why?** (I would feel very confused. I wouldn't believe what I saw because I know pandas can't sail boats.)

- **Pages 12–13** **What does the girl do?** (She takes a picture of the panda.) **Why does she do this?** (A photograph will help prove whether what she thinks she sees is really a panda.)

- **Pages 14–15** **Did the girl really see a panda? How do you know?** (Yes, she really saw a panda because the zoo says that a panda is missing.)

- **Page 16** **What else does the girl know?** (She knows that the zoo is missing a zebra because she took a picture of one.)

- **Page 16** **What is the big idea, or theme, of this book?** (We don't always believe what we see when our eyes see something surprising.)

Ongoing Assessment

Reading Strategies

If... a child makes errors while reading from page 12 to the end,	Then... have him or her slow down and read with a finger, since the words from here on are different from the pattern of earlier pages.
If... a child reads rhythmically and accurately,	Then... praise him or her for recognizing the rhythm and decoding words correctly.
If... a child has difficulty identifying the theme of the story,	Then... use **Model Your Thinking** below.

Model Your Thinking

 Comprehension Skill: Theme

Every story has a big idea, or theme. As I read, I think about what the big idea, or theme, of the story is. I ask myself: "What did the character learn? What can I learn from reading this story?" This story is about a girl who sees a panda. She says it can't be true. Then she keeps seeing the panda all around town. She still thinks it can't be true. Finally she takes a picture of the panda. The picture proves that she did see a panda. She learns that the zoo lost a panda. I think one big idea of this book is that we don't always believe what we see when our eyes see something surprising.

After Reading

Revisiting the Text

Comprehension Have children go through the book, telling what happens. Record each event using Web 1 on page 131. Be sure to include what the girl says. Then ask children to summarize the story. Guide children to discuss the theme of the story, which can be written in the center of the web.

30A
The Move

by Susan McCloskey
Leveled Reader 30A
Genre: Realistic Story
Level: Easy

Summary

It's moving day for an unhappy boy. He is going to miss his old house, his old school, and his friend Bill. But when he sees his new house and his new school and makes a new friend, he starts to change his mind. He also realizes that Bill can come over to his new house. Now the boy feels much better about the move.

Leveled Reader Practice

After children have read *The Move,* use Leveled Reader practice page 199 to assess their understanding of the Leveled Reader and the target comprehension skill. Additional after reading activities are provided on page 127.

At a Glance

Links to the Student Edition

☞ **Comprehension Skill:** Drawing Conclusions

Selection Vocabulary: *boy, school, move*

Program Theme: Creativity
Unit Theme: Surprise Me!

A young boy is surprised to discover that moving isn't as bad as it seems, especially if you can keep an old friend and make a new one.

Before Reading

Motivating the Reader
Build Background About Moving

Ask children if they have ever moved from one home to another. Ask them how they felt. Ask them what was hard about leaving an old home and what was hard about coming to a new one. Have children work in groups using the T-Chart on page 140. They can list good things and bad things about moving in the chart's columns. Tell children that they will read about a boy who is going through the process of moving.

Preview and Predict

Have children scan the cover, text, and illustrations. Encourage them to use picture clues and familiar words to predict what the book is about. Prepare children for reading by saying:

> Look at the picture on page 2. What is happening? How do you think the boy feels? Do you think his feelings will change? Read to find out what happens during the move.

Point out selection vocabulary and any unfamiliar words that are important to understanding the book, such as *please, miss,* and *supper.*

During Reading

Guiding Comprehension

Use the following questions to support children as they read.

- **Pages 2–3** How does the boy feel about having to move? How can you tell? (He is upset about the move. The boy looks unhappy. He says he doesn't want to move.) **What is one reason he gives for not having to move?** (He says the house is not too little.)

- **Pages 2–3** How would you feel if you were the boy? Why? (Encourage well-supported answers.)

- **Page 4** Why do you think the boy's parents want to move? How do you know? (They have a new baby and probably need a bigger house so there is room for everyone. The boy's words on pages 3 and 4 seem like his responses to problems his parents have mentioned.)

- **Page 5** What is another reason why the boy doesn't want to move? (He will miss his friend Bill.)

- **Page 6** Do you think the boy's idea to have Bill move with them is a good idea? Why or why not? (No. Bill's family would miss him if he moved. You usually don't have your friends move with you.)

- **Page 9** Do you think the boy is still upset about moving? Why or why not? (The boy seems less upset because he sees his new school and says that he likes it.)

- **Page 10** What else makes the boy feel differently about moving? (He likes the new house. He says Sam, his dog, likes it too.)

- **Pages 14–15** How does the boy feel now? What do you think he will do? (The boy is happy because he has a new house, a new school, and a new friend. But he still misses Bill. He'll find a way to see Bill.)

- **Page 16** How does the boy solve his problem? (He decides that Bill can come over and be friends with him and Jim.)

Reading Strategies

If... a child does not read with expression,	**Then...** point out end marks as clues and remind the child to read as if he or she were the boy talking.
If... a child notices the boy's negative feelings at the beginning of the book and his change of attitude toward the end,	**Then...** praise the child for paying close attention to story clues.
If... a child has difficulty drawing logical conclusions,	**Then...** use **Model Your Thinking** below.

Model Your Thinking

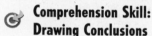 **Comprehension Skill: Drawing Conclusions**

 Think ALOUD

Sometimes authors don't tell me how a character feels or why something happens in a story. I can figure these things out for myself by thinking about what I've read and what I know about real life. For example, I can figure out from the boy's face on page 2 and his words that he is very upset by the move. I know that making a move can be difficult and scary. As I read, I'll pay attention to what the boy says and does to see if his feelings about the move change.

After Reading

Revisiting the Text

Comprehension Have small groups reread the book and complete the T-Chart on page 140. In the left column, they can list details about the boy and how he feels before moving. In the right column, they can list details about the boy and how he feels after the move. Have groups use their chart to role-play a conversation among the boy, Bill, and Jim that takes place after the move.

30B
Our Place

by Anne Phillips
Leveled Reader 30B
Genre: Narrative Nonfiction
Level: Easy/Average

Summary

Two children notice the places where different animals, such as a spider, a bird, a bee, a mouse, and a turtle, live. The story ends with the narrator stating that Earth is a place for us all.

Leveled Reader Practice

After children have read *Our Place,* use Leveled Reader practice page 200 to assess their understanding of the Leveled Reader and the target comprehension skill. Additional after reading activities are provided on page 129.

At a Glance

Links to the Student Edition

☞ **Comprehension Skill:** Drawing Conclusions

Selection Vocabulary: *open, always*

Program Theme: Creativity
Unit Theme: Surprise Me!

If we take a closer look, we may be surprised to see so many creatures living around us. If we take a look from far, far away, we'll see that Earth is a place where we all live.

Before Reading

Motivating the Reader
Build Background About Nature

Tell children that they will read a book that talks about the places different animals and plants live. Have them fill in the blanks in the following sentence. Write each completed sentence on the chalkboard.

A _____ is a place for a _____.

Give a model sentence if needed, such as: *A pond is a place for a fish.* Children can draw pictures to illustrate one or more of the completed sentences.

Preview and Predict

Have children scan the cover, text, and illustrations. Encourage them to use picture clues and familiar words to predict what the book is about. Prepare children for reading by saying:

> As you read, what animals do you see? What are the places for these animals? What do you think the title means by "our place"?

Suggest children read to find out if their predictions are correct.

Point out selection vocabulary and any unfamiliar words that are important to understanding the book, such as *place, twig, flies, flower, bush, garden,* and *pond.*

During Reading

● Guiding Comprehension

Use the following questions to support children as they read.

- **Page 2** *Where does a spider live?* (A spider lives on a web.)

- **Page 3** *Who eats flies for dinner?* (the spider)

- **Page 4** *Where do bird eggs belong?* (Eggs belong in a nest.) *What do you find in eggs?* (You find little birds in eggs.)

- **Page 5** *Who eats worms for dinner?* (the baby birds)

- **Page 6** *Where is a place for a garden?* (A yard is a place for a garden.) *Where is a place for a bee?* (A flower is a place for a bee.)

- **Page 7** *Who says these words? Why?* (The boy tells his sister not to smell the flower because there is a bee on the flower and his sister could get stung.)

- **Page 9** *What do rabbits like to eat?* (Rabbits like to eat carrots.)

- **Page 11** *Why does the boy tell the mouse to run away?* (A snake is coming, and snakes eat mice.)

- **Pages 12–13** *What places are mentioned on these pages? What is the animal?* (The places are a pond, a rock, and a shell, and the animal is a turtle.)

- **Pages 14–15** *What place do you think could be a place for all the things mentioned here?* (Answers may vary, but should describe a place larger than any of those mentioned.)

- **Page 16** *Where is a place for us all?* (Earth is a place for us all.)

Reading Strategies

If... a child stumbles on words such as *web* on page 2, *garden* or *flower* on page 6, or *bush* on page 8,

Then... suggest that the child begin with the letters and sounds, but also use picture clues to figure out the word.

If... a child has difficulty drawing logical conclusions,

Then... use **Model Your Thinking** below.

Model Your Thinking

 Comprehension Skill: Drawing Conclusions

 Think ALOUD

Authors don't always tell us everything about what happens in a story. Good readers use clues from the story and what they know about real life to figure out things the author may not tell them. For example, I read the words "Flies for dinner!" on page 3, and I wonder who eats flies for dinner. I look at the picture and think about what I know about spiders. I figure out that the spider will eat flies for dinner.

After Reading

Revisiting the Text

Comprehension Have children reread the book and choose any left-hand page from 2 to 12. They can draw and label a picture to match the text. Ask children whether the text starts with the smallest or the largest of the three things mentioned. Ask them to draw a conclusion about the pattern in the book, and write the children's conclusion on the chalkboard. Then reread pages 14–16 together. Guide children to conclude that the answer is Earth because it's big enough for all the places and animals mentioned in the story.

Name _____

Book Title _____

Read the title. Look at the pictures.

Draw a picture or write about one problem in the story.

© Scott Foresman 1

© Scott Foresman 1

© Scott Foresman 1

Topic _____

What We K now

What We W ant to Know

What We L earned

© Scott Foresman 1

Name _____

Book Title _____

Beginning

Middle

End

© Scott Foresman 1

© Scott Foresman 1

Main Idea

Details

© Scott Foresman 1

Problem

Solution

© Scott Foresman 1

© Scott Foresman 1

1

2

3

4

5

© Scott Foresman 1

© Scott Foresman 1

☞ Context Clues

Read the story *Come Back!* Then answer Numbers 1 through 5.

1 This story tells how the dog

- ○ looks for the animals.
- ○ met a big pig.
- ○ sits in the sun.

☞ **2** Look at page 2. The dog looks for the

- ○ cats.
- ○ pigs.
- ○ hens.

☞ **3** Look at page 5. The dog thinks the pigs

- ○ dug in the mud.
- ○ ran away.
- ○ took a nap.

4 Look at page 7. How does the dog feel?

- ○ sad
- ○ happy
- ○ mad

5 Where did they all go? Draw a picture.

© Scott Foresman 1

Context Clues

Read the story *Tex Has an Itch*. Then answer Numbers 1 through 5.

1 Why does Tex want help?

   ○ Tex has a cut.
   ○ Tex has an itch.
   ○ Tex has a bad back.

2 Look at page 3. Who does Tex hope will help?

   ○ Horse
   ○ Bear
   ○ Dog

3 What tells about Horse and Bob?

   ○ Horse and Bob need help.
   ○ Horse and Bob help Tex.
   ○ Horse and Bob do not help Tex.

4 Horse and Bob may think Tex will

   ○ jab them.
   ○ help them.
   ○ fan them.

5 Read the sentences about the story. Draw a picture for them.

Bird helps Tex. Bird will fix the itch.

© Scott Foresman 1

☞ Cause and Effect

Read the story *Come and Play*. Then answer Numbers 1 through 5.

1 What does the boy want to do?

- ○ jog
- ○ play
- ○ dig

☞ **2** Look at pages 4 and 5. The boy sees Frog. What happens?

- ○ Frog hops on a rock.
- ○ Frog pats Dog.
- ○ Frog gets on top of Cat.

3 Look at pages 5 and 6. What does Butterfly do?

- ○ Butterfly comes down.
- ○ Butterfly goes away.
- ○ Butterfly sits in the tree.

4 Look at page 7. How many animals does the boy have?

- ○ five
- ○ six
- ○ four

☞ **5** The boy had too many animals. Draw a picture of what happened.

© Scott Foresman 1

Name _____

☞ Cause and Effect

Read the story *Paper Fun*. Then answer Numbers 1 through 5.

☞ **1** The boy can NOT find his plane. What happens?

   ○ The girl makes a plane.
   ○ The girl sees a plane.
   ○ The girls finds the plane.

2 Look at page 5. What will the girl make?

   ○ a pail
   ○ a rope
   ○ a boat

☞ **3** Look at page 8. The boy is NOT happy. Why?

   ○ The boy can not jump.
   ○ The boy can not see.
   ○ The boy can not play.

4 Look at page 8. The hat is too

   ○ little.
   ○ red.
   ○ big.

5 Draw pictures of the things the girl made.

© Scott Foresman 1

⟳ Predicting

Read the story *Who Went Up?* Then answer Numbers 1 through 5.

1 What happens to the bugs in this story?

○ They play ball.
○ They get wet.
○ They go up.

⟳ 2 Look at page 5. Who went up?

○ the bug with the ball
○ the bug with a hat
○ the bug with the balloon

3 Look at page 8. How does the bug feel?

○ sad
○ glad
○ mad

⟳ 4 Look at page 8. What might happen next?

○ A dog will go up.
○ A pig will go up.
○ Bugs will come down.

5 How do the three bugs go up? Draw pictures of the bugs.

© Scott Foresman 1

☞ Predicting

Read the story *Go Away, Bugs!* Then answer Numbers 1 through 5.

① The bugs in this story can

- ○ swim.
- ○ hide.
- ○ hum.

② Why do the bugs go away?

- ○ The bird might eat them.
- ○ The bugs want to play.
- ○ The bird might hop on them.

③ Look at page 6. Why can the bark go up?

- ○ It is a bird.
- ○ It is a plane.
- ○ It is a bug.

☞ **④** Look at page 7. The leaf is a bug. How can you tell?

- ○ The leaf has legs.
- ○ The leaf is green and little.
- ○ The tree is a good home.

☞ **⑤** Look at page 8. What may happen next? Draw a picture.

© Scott Foresman 1

☞ Setting

Read the story *How Many on the Log?* Then answer Numbers 1 through 5.

☞ **1** This story happens in the

   ○ fall.
   ○ spring.
   ○ winter.

2 Look at page 5. Next there will be five frogs on the log. How can you tell?

   ○ Five comes after four.
   ○ The frogs look happy.
   ○ The frogs like to sit.

3 Look at page 7. How many frogs are on the log?

   ○ five
   ○ six
   ○ seven

4 Why do the frogs hop off the log?

   ○ The frogs are hot.
   ○ The frogs want to swim.
   ○ The frogs see a cat.

☞ **5** Where do the frogs live? Draw a picture.

© Scott Foresman 1

☞ Setting

Read the story _With the Fish_. Then answer Numbers 1 through 5.

1 Look at page 4. Tim saw

    ○ little fish.
    ○ yellow fish.
    ○ blue fish.

2 How are the fish ALIKE?

    ○ They can hide.
    ○ They can play.
    ○ They can walk.

3 Why are the children happy?

    ○ They can go home.
    ○ They can swim.
    ○ They like to see fish.

☞ **4** Look at each page. The children see fish and

    ○ plants.
    ○ ducks.
    ○ trees.

☞ **5** Where do the fish live? Draw a picture.

© Scott Foresman 1

☞ Author's Purpose

Read the story *Jack and Jill*. Then answer Numbers 1 through 5.

1 Jack and Jill are

  ○ little bugs.
  ○ little frogs.
  ○ big bears.

2 Jack and Jill go up the hill

  ○ to play in the water.
  ○ to look in the well.
  ○ to get a pail of water.

☞ **3** This story

  ○ makes you laugh.
  ○ tells you about real frogs.
  ○ makes you frown.

☞ **4** This story was

  ○ sad.
  ○ real.
  ○ funny.

5 What happens AFTER Jack and Jill fall down? Draw a picture.

© Scott Foresman 1

☞ Author's Purpose

Read the story *In and Out*. Then answer Numbers 1 through 5.

1 This story happens

- ○ in the day.
- ○ when the sun is up.
- ○ at night.

2 Where does the raccoon find food?

- ○ in a garden
- ○ in a can
- ○ in a tree

3 The raccoon does NOT go into

- ○ a log.
- ○ a shed.
- ○ a pen.

☞ **4** This story

- ○ tells about real animals.
- ○ makes you feel sad.
- ○ makes you want a pet.

☞ **5** The end of the story is a surprise. Draw a picture of the surprise.

© Scott Foresman 1

ℰ Cause and Effect

Read the story *Stop! Eat!* Then answer Numbers 1 through 5.

1 This story tells what animals

○ make.
○ see.
○ eat.

2 The mom tells her babies to

○ Stop! Eat!
○ Go! Play!
○ Stop! Walk!

ℰ **3** The animals find a tree. What happens?

○ They sit by the tree.
○ They eat the leaves.
○ They go up the tree.

ℰ **4** Look at page 8. Why do the animals stop?

○ The animals ate the food.
○ They want to go to sleep.
○ They see the light.

5 Look at page 8. What might happen next? Draw a picture.

© Scott Foresman 1

☞ Cause and Effect

Read the story *Night Songs*. Then answer Numbers 1 through 5.

1 Look at page 2. What time of day is it?

○ lunch time
○ bed time
○ day time

2 This story happens

○ on a farm.
○ at the zoo.
○ on a bus.

3 Who sings by night?

○ owls and frogs
○ dogs and cats
○ Mom and the boy

☞ **4** Look at page 8. Why does the boy look out?

○ He wants to see his dad.
○ He wants to go to sleep.
○ He wants to hear them sing.

☞ **5** The boy hears them sing. How does the boy feel now? Draw a picture.

© Scott Foresman 1

Compare and Contrast

Read the story *Goal!* Then answer Numbers 1 through 5.

1 Who wants help?

- ○ Tim
- ○ Kit
- ○ Tomas

2 How are Tim and Kit ALIKE?

- ○ They do not like to play
- ○ They like to play.
- ○ They ask for help.

3 How is Kit NOT like Tim?

- ○ Kit is not wearing socks.
- ○ Kit is not on the grass.
- ○ Kit is not on Tim's team.

4 How does the story end?

- ○ Tim gets the ball.
- ○ Tim kicks the ball in the net.
- ○ Kit kicks the ball in the net.

5 What does Tim like to do? Draw a picture.

© Scott Foresman 1

☞ Compare and Contrast

Read the story _This Means Stop_. Then answer Numbers 1 through 5.

❶ Look at page 2. Who can stop ☞ now?

- ○ the yellow cab
- ○ the boy and the mom
- ○ the yellow cab, the boy, and the mom

❷ Look at page 4. What can the car do?

- ○ turn
- ○ stop
- ○ go slow

❸ Look at page 5. How are the cars ALIKE?

- ○ They can go slow.
- ○ They are green.
- ○ They must stop.

❹ Look at page 6. Who can go now?

- ○ the cars
- ○ the boy and his mom
- ○ the boy

☞ **❺** Draw two pictures. Draw a hand that means _STOP_. Draw hands that mean _GO_.

© Scott Foresman 1

↻ Drawing Conclusions

Read the story *Hic! Hic! Hic!* Then answer Numbers 1 through 5.

1 This story tells how the animals

○ dig holes.
○ play tag.
○ find holes.

2 What do the animals hear?

○ Hic! Hic! Hic!
○ Stop! Stop! Stop!
○ Help! Help! Help!

3 Look at page 7. You can tell the animals feel

○ happy.
○ scared.
○ sad.

↻ **4** Who made the holes?

○ the mole
○ Pat
○ the leaf

↻ **5** What will happen if Pat holds a balloon? Draw a picture.

© Scott Foresman 1

☞ Drawing Conclusions

Read the story *Oh, Good!* Then answer Numbers 1 through 5.

1 The big sister does NOT want

- ○ all of her games.
- ○ her old things.
- ○ her good toys.

2 Look at page 6. The big sister does NOT want the shirt because

- ○ it is too small.
- ○ it is too big.
- ○ it is not hers.

☞ **3** Look at page 14. How does the little sister feel?

- ○ silly
- ○ happy
- ○ sad

☞ **4** Look at page 16. What do the sisters like the BEST?

- ○ to share things
- ○ to sit under a table
- ○ to take a nap

5 Look at page 16. What might happen next? Draw a picture.

© Scott Foresman 1

☞ Main Idea

Read the story *Jump Rope Time*. Then answer Numbers 1 through 5.

☞ **1** What BEST tells what this story is about?

- ○ playing ball
- ○ helping Tim and Jan
- ○ jumping rope

2 How are Jan and Tim ALIKE?

- ○ They are not good at jumping rope.
- ○ They are good at jumping rope.
- ○ They are good at playing tag.

3 Look at page 8. The girl turns the rope and jumps. What happens?

- ○ She misses.
- ○ She falls.
- ○ She runs away.

☞ **4** Look at page 15. The girl can jump rope now. Why?

- ○ She has a good rope.
- ○ She rested on the swing.
- ○ She jumped and jumped.

5 Look at the story pictures. Who is with the girl all the time? Draw a picture.

© Scott Foresman 1

⚘ Main Idea

Read the story *Sleepy Pig*. Then answer Numbers 1 through 5.

⚘ ❶ What BEST tells what this story is about?

- ○ a happy duck
- ○ a little puppy
- ○ a sleeping pig

⚘ ❷ Pig sleeps when the animals

- ○ play.
- ○ work.
- ○ sleep.

❸ What tells about Pig?

- ○ Pig will not help.
- ○ Pig likes to work.
- ○ Pig wants to dig.

❹ Look at page 12. What do Bob and Dan have in the bags?

- ○ dirt
- ○ food
- ○ eggs

❺ Look at page 14. What does Pig want to do? Draw a picture.

© Scott Foresman 1

☛ Classifying

Read the story *Molly and Polly*. Then answer Numbers 1 through 5.

1 Molly tells Polly how to

- ○ eat.
- ○ talk.
- ○ sing.

2 Molly gives Polly a cracker. Why?

- ○ Polly wants to eat.
- ○ Polly can say *cracker*.
- ○ Polly likes to flap her wings.

3 Look at page 9. What do Molly and Dad think?

- ○ The dog wants to eat.
- ○ The bell is ringing.
- ○ The dog is talking.

☛ **4** Who can talk in this story?

- ○ the dog, Polly, Molly
- ○ Molly, Polly, Dad
- ○ Polly, Dad, the dog

☛ **5** What pets does Molly have? Draw a picture.

© Scott Foresman 1

☞ Classifying

Read the story *The Zookeeper*. Then answer Numbers 1 through 5.

☞ **1** All the animals in the story live

○ on a farm.
○ at the zoo.
○ in the water.

2 This story tells you

○ where animals like to hide.
○ when animals go to sleep.
○ what animals like to eat.

☞ **3** Some big animals in the story are

○ the bear, elephant, and giraffe.
○ the fox, monkey, and elephant.
○ the giraffe, bear, and fox.

4 Look at page 16. Why does the zookeeper love her job?

○ She likes to work with animals.
○ She likes to eat.
○ She likes to carry a pail.

5 Draw a picture of an animal from the story. Show what it likes to eat.

© Scott Foresman 1

Context Clues

Read the story *Wash Day*. Then answer Numbers 1 through 5.

1 Look at page 2. What does the boy get?

- ○ sun
- ○ soap
- ○ rope

2 Why does the boy get a tub?

- ○ He wants to wash his bike.
- ○ He needs to take a bath.
- ○ He wants to wash his dog.

3 Look at page 7. What does Pam get?

- ○ a rake
- ○ a bug
- ○ a bike

4 Who gets the chairs and the car?

- ○ Pam and the boy
- ○ Mama and Papa
- ○ The boy and Mama

5 Look at page 14. They wash things all day. What happens to them? Draw a picture.

© Scott Foresman 1

Context Clues

Read the story *Looking for the Queen*. Then answer Numbers 1 through 5.

1 Look at pages 4 and 5. Who are they looking for?

  ○ the king
  ○ the queen
  ○ a man

2 Look at page 6. What does she have for the queen?

  ○ letters
  ○ books
  ○ a mop

3 Where is the queen?

  ○ in her bed
  ○ in the pool
  ○ in a jet

4 Look at page 15. They see the queen having fun. What do they do next?

  ○ They do the jobs.
  ○ They go away.
  ○ They get in the pool.

5 Draw a picture for this sentence.

  The queen is having fun.

© Scott Foresman 1

☞ Character

Read the story *Do What I Do*. Then answer Numbers 1 through 5.

1 Look at page 3. What does the girl want to do?

○ teach the pig how to dance
○ dance with all her pets
○ read a book to the pig

☞ **2** Look at page 9. The pig falls on the girl. What happens next?

○ The girl gets mad and goes away.
○ The pig gets mad and goes away.
○ They get up and dance again.

☞ **3** Look at page 14. You can tell the pig and the girl feel

○ mad.
○ happy.
○ sad.

4 Look at page 15. What does the pig like to do now?

○ The pig likes to sleep.
○ The pig likes to talk.
○ The pig likes to dance.

☞ **5** How do the girl and the pig feel AFTER they dance? Draw a picture.

© Scott Foresman 1

Name

☞ Character

Read the story *Peas Please*. Then answer Numbers 1 through 5.

1 Look at pages 2 and 3. The boy wants his sister to

  ○ go to sleep.
  ○ eat peas.
  ○ get a bib.

☞ 2 The boy is nice. He says

  ○ please!
  ○ no!
  ○ stop!

3 Look at page 13. What does the baby want to do?

  ○ play with her toy
  ○ eat the peas
  ○ clap her hands

4 Look at page 16. The baby thinks the boy is

  ○ big.
  ○ happy.
  ○ funny.

☞ 5 The baby does not want to eat. What does the baby do? Draw a picture.

© Scott Foresman 1

Name _____

☞ Realism and Fantasy

Read the story _Jump, Jump_. Then answer Numbers 1 through 5.

❶ What BEST tells what this story is about?

- ○ playing with Baby
- ○ jumping rope
- ○ watching the dog

❷ Who can NOT jump rope?

- ○ Mom and Dad
- ○ Sister and Brother
- ○ Baby and the dog

❸ What happens AFTER Baby jumps in?

- ○ Baby is fast, fast, fast.
- ○ They all fall down.
- ○ Sister helps Baby jump.

☞ **❹** This story

- ○ could happen in real life.
- ○ could make you mad.
- ○ could not happen in real life.

☞ **❺** Look at page 16. What could happen next? Draw a picture.

© Scott Foresman 1

☞ Realism and Fantasy

Read the story *Biff Helps After All*. Then answer Numbers 1 through 5.

1 Look at pages 2 and 3. Who is the boy talking to?

○ his mom
○ his dog
○ his cat

2 What does the boy want to do?

○ He wants to make his bike look good.
○ He wants to get a new red bike.
○ He wants his dog to ride his bike.

3 Look at pages 12 and 13. What does Biff do?

○ Biff rides the bike.
○ Biff runs down the street.
○ Biff runs with the red ribbon.

☞ **4** This story

○ could not happen in real life.
○ could happen in real life.
○ could make you feel sad.

☞ **5** What if Biff was NOT a real dog. What could Biff do? Draw a picture.

© Scott Foresman 1

☞ Theme

Read the story *Mother's Day*. Then answer Numbers 1 through 5.

1 When does this story happen?

- ○ at lunch
- ○ at night
- ○ on Mother's Day

☞ 2 What is this story about?

- ○ Kitty makes breakfast for Mom.
- ○ Kitty learns how to cook lunch.
- ○ Kitty wants to eat some breakfast.

☞ 3 Look at pages 2 and 3. Who made the sign on the wall?

- ○ Mom
- ○ Kitty
- ○ Dad

4 The cats in this story are NOT real. How do you know?

- ○ Real cats do not make food.
- ○ Real cats have tails.
- ○ Real cats can live in a house.

5 Look at page 16. What might happen next? Draw a picture.

© Scott Foresman 1

Name _____

Theme

Read the story *Where Bat Came From*. Then answer Numbers 1 through 5.

1 What does Mouse do with his friends?

   ○ play ball
   ○ take a walk
   ○ work all day

2 What can Mouse do?

   ○ kick
   ○ catch
   ○ jump

3 Look at pages 12 and 13. How does Mother Mouse help Mouse?

   ○ She tells him to jump again and again.
   ○ She takes the ball away.
   ○ She turns into a bat.

4 What happens to mouse AFTER he jumps and jumps?

   ○ He jumps on his mother.
   ○ He turns into a bat.
   ○ He turns into a ball.

5 What can Bat do? Draw a picture.

© Scott Foresman 1

☞ Main Idea

Read the story *A Day for Dad*. Then answer Numbers 1 through 5.

1 Why does Ben let Dad sleep late?

○ Ben wants to play.
○ It is Father's Day.
○ Ben can not tell time.

2 Why does Ben wash Dad's car?

○ Ben thinks the car is a mess.
○ Ben wants to play in water.
○ Ben thinks Dad will like it.

☞ **3** What gift does Dad like BEST?

○ the hug
○ the car
○ the cat

☞ **4** What BEST tells what this story is about?

○ Ben is nice to his dad.
○ Ben makes a card.
○ Ben helps his mom.

☞ **5** Ben makes gifts for Dad. Draw a picture that shows one of the gifts.

© Scott Foresman 1

☞ Main Idea

Read the story *Karate Class*. Then answer Numbers 1 through 5.

☞ ❶ What BEST tells what this story is about?

- ○ Linn goes to karate class.
- ○ Linn yells in class.
- ○ Linn wears a white belt.

❷ How does Linn feel about karate class?

- ○ She does not like karate class.
- ○ She is going to karate class.
- ○ She loves karate class.

❸ What does Linn do at karate class?

- ○ She jumps and runs.
- ○ She sings and dances.
- ○ She kicks and chops.

❹ Look at page 15. It is the end of class. What does the bow mean?

- ○ It is time to go.
- ○ I am ready.
- ○ Thank you for the class.

☞ ❺ Linn does many things at karate class. Draw a picture of one thing Linn does.

© Scott Foresman 1

☞ Author's Purpose

Read the story *Be There!* Then answer Numbers 1 through 5.

1 Look at page 2. Where will they go?

   ○ to Gram's house
   ○ to the fair
   ○ on a trip

2 Look at pages 8 and 9. How are the Pet Show and T-Ball ALIKE?

   ○ They have pretty animals.
   ○ They have bats and balls.
   ○ They happen from 2–4 p.m.

☞ **3** What does this story help you do?

   ○ It helps you tell time.
   ○ It helps you run in a race.
   ○ It helps you play with friends.

☞ **4** Look at page 16. What do the words *THE END* tell you?

   ○ It is the end of the day and the book.
   ○ It is the end of the road.
   ○ It is the end of the dance.

5 Look at page 10. What time is it? Draw a picture of a clock with that time on it.

© Scott Foresman 1

☞ Author's Purpose

Read the story *Zulu Dancer*. Then answer Numbers 1 through 5.

☞ **1** This story tells you

- ○ how to kick your feet.
- ○ about Zulu dancers.
- ○ where to go to school.

2 Who is a Zulu dancer in this story?

- ○ the boy
- ○ the brother
- ○ the father

3 How does a Zulu dancer dance?

- ○ fast and hard
- ○ fast and slow
- ○ soft and hard

☞ **4** Look at pages 14 and 15. What does the author tell us about the boy?

- ○ He thinks about holding a stick.
- ○ He thinks about running in the dirt.
- ○ He thinks about being a dancer.

5 When the boy is bigger, he will be a Zulu dancer. What will he look like? Draw a picture.

© Scott Foresman 1

☛ Plot

Read the story *The Three Bears*. Then answer Numbers 1 through 5.

☛ **1** Three brown bears live in a house with

- ○ three lamps, three rugs, and three sinks.
- ○ four bowls, four chairs, and four beds.
- ○ three bowls, three chairs, and three beds.

2 Look at page 7. The three bears are surprised. Why?

- ○ They count four bowls, four chairs, and four beds.
- ○ Someone is sleeping in Baby Bear's bed.
- ○ They see a Papa, Mama, and Baby Bear.

☛ **3** Look at pages 12 and 13. Who is sleeping in the four beds?

- ○ four bears
- ○ four rabbits
- ○ a little girl

☛ **4** Look at pages 12 and 13. What do the three brown bears know now?

- ○ They have to take a nap.
- ○ This is not where they live.
- ○ They will have four friends.

☛ **5** Look at page 16. What will happen next? Draw a picture.

© Scott Foresman 1

☞ Plot

Read the story *Long Tom*. Then answer Numbers 1 through 5.

❶ What can you tell about this story?

- ○ It could happen in real life.
- ○ It could not happen in real life.
- ○ It could be sad to read.

❷ What is Long Tom's job?

- ○ to scare the animals away
- ○ to help the animals eat corn
- ○ to play with cans and plates

☞❸ Look at pages 10 and 11. Why does Long Tom feel sad?

- ○ He can not flap, flap.
- ○ The sun is going down.
- ○ He is all alone.

☞❹ At the end of the story, what do the animals do?

- ○ They scare Long Tom away.
- ○ They help Long Tom to fly.
- ○ They eat all the corn.

❺ What animals were eating the corn? Draw a picture.

© Scott Foresman 1

↻ Realism and Fantasy

Read the story *Knock-Knock Jokes*. Then answer Numbers 1 through 5.

1 What do the chimps like to do?

○ swing on branches
○ live at the zoo
○ tell knock-knock jokes

2 The chimps tell jokes about

○ pets.
○ fruit.
○ fish.

↻ **3** What can real chimps do?

○ Real chimps can eat fruit.
○ Real chimps can talk.
○ Real chimps can paint pictures.

4 Look at page 16. What does the little chimp want to make?

○ a fruit salad
○ one more painting
○ some strawberry jam

↻ **5** Think about the story. What could NOT happen in real life? Draw a picture.

© Scott Foresman 1

Realism and Fantasy

Read the story *The First Day of Winter*. Then answer Numbers 1 through 5.

1 What does Bunny need to do to go out?

○ He needs to read a book.
○ He needs to dress warm.
○ He needs to take a bath.

2 This story could NOT happen in real life. Why?

○ A bunny goes outside in this story.
○ A bunny talks in this story.
○ A bunny looks cute in this story.

3 Look at page 16. Bunny can NOT get up. Why?

○ He wants to play on the floor.
○ He can not find his shoes.
○ He is wearing too many things.

4 What can a real bunny do?

○ put on socks
○ tie a scarf
○ eat a leaf

5 Look at page 16. What can happen next? Draw a picture.

© Scott Foresman 1

↻ Predicting

Read the story *That Is Right, Walrus*. Then answer Numbers 1 through 5.

1 Walrus does NOT go

- ○ to the playground.
- ○ to the beach.
- ○ to Grandma's house.

2 Look at page 7. Walrus should buy cowboy boots. Why?

- ○ She is going to a cold place.
- ○ She is going to a ranch.
- ○ She is going to the beach.

↻ **3** Look at page 11. Will Walrus think of the bed or the sleeping bag first ?

- ○ She will think of the bed first.
- ○ She will think of the sleeping bag first.
- ○ She will ask her Grandma first.

4 What is the right gift for Grandma?

- ○ flowers
- ○ a book
- ○ a book and flowers

↻ **5** Look at page 2. How do you know Walrus will buy the bathing suit?

_____

_____

_____

_____

© Scott Foresman 1

☞ Predicting

Read the story *Texas Eggs*. Then answer Numbers 1 through 5.

1 Look at pages 2 and 3. How did the girl get to Texas?

○ by boat
○ by plane
○ by car

☞ 2 Look at page 11. How do you know Grandpa will play with the shell next?

○ Grandpa played with the shells on the other days.
○ Grandpa likes to play with things to eat.
○ All grandpas use shells for fun.

3 Why does Grandpa save the shells?

○ He fills the shells with bits of paper.
○ He wants to give them to the cat.
○ He makes pictures with the shells.

4 The girl breaks the shell over Grandpa's head. What happens?

○ Grandpa gets mad.
○ The children stop playing.
○ The bits of paper fall on Grandpa.

☞ 5 The girl asks, **"Why do you want the shells?"** What will Grandpa say next? Write the words from the story.

_____

_____

_____

_____

© Scott Foresman 1

Compare and Contrast

Read the story *From Dad*. Then answer Numbers 1 through 5.

1 When the girl was five, her dad gave her

○ a panda.
○ a hug.
○ a T-shirt.

2 How were things ALIKE each year?

○ The girl wore the T-shirt.
○ The girl wore blue shoes.
○ The girl is little.

3 How old is the girl at the end of the story?

○ five
○ six
○ seven

4 The T-shirt does not fit. What does the girl do?

○ She gives it to her sister.
○ She puts it on her panda.
○ She throws it in the trash.

5 Look at page 3. Then look at page 11. How is the girl DIFFERENT? Use words from the story in your answer.

_____

_____

_____

_____

_____

_____

_____

© Scott Foresman 1

☞ Compare and Contrast

Read the book *House of Wood, House of Snow.* **Then answer Numbers 1 through 5.**

☞ **1** BOTH houses have

- ○ walls, sinks, stoves, tables.
- ○ windows, doors, lamps, beds.
- ○ steps, tables, lamps, tubs.

2 Who makes the igloo?

- ○ the father
- ○ the mother
- ○ everyone

3 How long does it take to make an igloo?

- ○ six hours
- ○ three days
- ○ three hours

☞ **4** How does the girl feel about the two houses?

- ○ She likes to live in both houses.
- ○ She likes the igloo best.
- ○ She wants one more wood house.

☞ **5** How are the two houses ALIKE? Use words from the book in your answer.

_____

– – – – – – – – – – – – – – – – – – –

_____

– – – – – – – – – – – – – – – – – – –

_____

– – – – – – – – – – – – – – – – – – –

© Scott Foresman 1

☞ Sequence of Events

Read the story *Mary Goes Walking*. Then answer Numbers 1 through 5.

☞ **1** What happens FIRST in the story?

  ○ Mary gets dressed up.
  ○ Mary goes out to play.
  ○ Mary plays with her cat.

☞ **2** What happens AFTER Mary gets dressed up?

  ○ Mary goes to a dance.
  ○ Mary goes for a walk.
  ○ Mary goes shopping.

3 Why does Mary lean over the water?

  ○ to get a drink
  ○ to see her cat
  ○ to see how she looks

4 What happens when Mary leans over the water?

  ○ Mary sees a bug in the water.
  ○ Mary falls in the water.
  ○ Mary jumps over the water.

☞ **5** What happens LAST in the story? Use words from the story in your answer.

_____

- -

_____

- -

_____

- -

© Scott Foresman 1

☞ Sequence of Events

Read the book *Desert Fox*. Then answer Numbers 1 through 5.

1 This book tells you about

○ a fox in a cage.
○ a fox in zoo.
○ a fox in the desert.

2 What does the fox need?

○ food and water
○ rocks and plants
○ mom and dad

3 What does the fox do when the sun goes down?

○ She goes to sleep.
○ She wakes up.
○ She drinks some water.

☞ **4** The old fox sees a lizard. What does she do FIRST?

○ She calls the lizard.
○ She looks and waits.
○ She runs around.

☞ **5** What happens LAST in the book? Use words from the book in your answer.

_____

_____

_____

_____

_____

_____

© Scott Foresman 1

⟳ Cause and Effect

Read the story *All Together Now!* Then answer Numbers 1 through 5.

❶ Look at page 2. Where is the family going?

- ○ They are going camping.
- ○ They are going on a trip.
- ○ They are going on a walk.

⟳ ❷ What happens when the family sees bugs?

- ○ They slap the bugs.
- ○ They spray the bugs.
- ○ They catch the bugs.

⟳ ❸ Look at pages 14 and 15. Why does the family run away?

- ○ They see a bear.
- ○ They see a skunk.
- ○ They see tracks.

❹ The family does NOT see

- ○ a snake on the walk.
- ○ a deer on the walk.
- ○ a hawk on the walk.

⟳ ❺ Look at page 7. Why does the sister hold her brother's arm? Use words from the story in your answer.

_____

- -

_____

- -

_____

- -

_____

- -

_____

- -

© Scott Foresman 1

☞ Cause and Effect

Read the story *How Bill Found Rain*. Then answer Numbers 1 through 5.

☞ **1** Why does the family need rain?

- ○ The animals drank all the water.
- ○ It has been too hot and dry.
- ○ Sis has a new raincoat.

2 Why does Bill look for a big black cloud?

- ○ Rain comes from big black clouds.
- ○ He can not pull a white cloud home.
- ○ Bill only likes black clouds.

☞ **3** Look at page 15. Bill pulls hard on the rope. What happens?

- ○ The dog starts to bark.
- ○ Mom starts to laugh.
- ○ It starts to rain.

4 What could NOT happen?

- ○ It could not be hot and sunny.
- ○ People could not find lots of rope.
- ○ A boy could not catch a cloud with a rope.

☞ **5** Look at page 16. Why is everyone dancing? Use words from the story in your answer.

_____

_____

_____

_____

© Scott Foresman 1

Main Idea

Read the book *Pandas*. Then answer Numbers 1 through 5.

1 This book tells about

- ○ teddy bears.
- ○ *The Three Bears*.
- ○ real pandas.

2 Where do pandas live?

- ○ in China
- ○ in water
- ○ on a farm

3 Look at page 5. What does the word *habits* mean?

- ○ what an animal family looks like
- ○ things an animal does again and again
- ○ the places where animals live

4 What BEST tells what this book is about?

- ○ things pandas like to do
- ○ how pandas like to sleep
- ○ things pandas like to eat

5 What do pandas like to do? Write about one thing they do. Use words from the book in your answer.

_____

_____

_____

_____

_____

© Scott Foresman 1

⌖ Main Idea

Read the story *What Lilly Pup Heard*. Then answer Numbers 1 through 5.

⌖ **1** What BEST tells what this story is about?

    ○ Lilly Pup can not find a quiet place to read at home.

    ○ Lilly Pup gets lost in the woods.

    ○ Lilly Pup wants her mother to read.

2 Where does Lilly Pup go to read?

    ○ to her school

    ○ to her grandma's house

    ○ to a quiet spot

3 What happens AFTER Lilly Pup reads most of her book?

    ○ She goes back home.

    ○ She goes to sleep.

    ○ She plays a game.

4 Why does Lilly Pup wake up?

    ○ She hears her family looking for her.

    ○ She hears her dog barking.

    ○ She hears a bird tweeting.

⌖ **5** What does Lilly Pup like to do MOST? Use words from the story in your answer.

_____

_____

_____

_____

_____

© Scott Foresman 1

ℭ Cause and Effect

Read the story *Why Little Possum's Tail Is Bare*. Then answer Numbers 1 through 5.

1 This is a make-believe story that tells

○ why possums run from cats.

○ why bees sting.

○ why possums have bare tails.

2 This story teaches us that

○ we should listen to our mothers.

○ we should stay away from possums.

○ we should try to see everything.

ℭ **3** Little Possum gets too close to the fire. What happens?

○ The fire goes out.

○ The fire burns his tail.

○ The fire burns his ears.

ℭ **4** The story tells us that all possums have bare tails because

○ Little Possum had to see the bees.

○ Little Possum listened to his mother.

○ Little Possum got too close to the fire.

ℭ **5** Little Possum puts his nose in the beehive. What happens? Use story words in your answer.

_____

- -

_____

- -

_____

- -

_____

© Scott Foresman 1

☞ Cause and Effect

Read the story *Many Little Beads*. Then answer Numbers 1 through 5.

1 Who made Robin's bracelet?

○ a girl who works at the mall

○ a girl who lives far away

○ a woman who lives down the street

☞ **2** Look at pages 6 and 7. Why does the woman buy the bracelet?

○ She wants to wear it.

○ She wants to sell it.

○ She likes the many little beads.

3 What does the woman do with the bracelet?

○ She sends it to Robin.

○ She keeps it in a bag.

○ She wears it every day.

4 Who sent the bracelet to Robin?

○ her mother's sister

○ her mother

○ her dad

☞ **5** What happens when Robin looks at her bracelet? Use words from the story in your answer.

_____

_____

_____

_____

_____

© Scott Foresman 1

Name _____

⌕ Sequence of Events

Read the book _Wish Faces: Face Painting Fun_. Then answer Numbers 1 through 5.

1 This book tells you

- ○ how to paint your face.
- ○ how to paint a picture.
- ○ how to use a brush.

2 How can you be funny?

- ○ Paint your face like a cat.
- ○ Paint your face like a clown.
- ○ Paint your face like a zebra.

⌕ **3** You want to paint a face. FIRST you will

- ○ get your friend.
- ○ get a brush, water, and paint.
- ○ hop on the ground.

4 Why do you need to make a drawing of what you want to be?

- ○ It shows how a bunny hops.
- ○ It keeps the table neat and clean.
- ○ It helps you see how to paint the face.

⌕ **5** You want to paint a face. What is the LAST step? Use words from the book in your answer.

_____

_____

_____

_____

© Scott Foresman 1

☞ Sequence of Events

Read the book *The Toymaker*. Then answer Numbers 1 through 5.

1 What is Bill's job?

- ○ an airplane pilot
- ○ a toymaker
- ○ a house painter

2 The pictures in this book are taken in

- ○ a kitchen.
- ○ a barn.
- ○ a workshop.

☞ **3** Bill makes a toy. FIRST, he

- ○ draws a picture of the new toy.
- ○ cleans up his workshop.
- ○ paints the new toy.

4 What toy does Bill make in this book?

- ○ a doll
- ○ an airplane
- ○ a boat

☞ **5** What does Bill do AFTER he paints the new toy? Use words from the book in your answer.

_____

- -

_____

- -

_____

- -

_____

- -

_____

- -

_____

© Scott Foresman 1

☞ Theme

Read the story *Look at Him Go!* Then answer Numbers 1 through 5.

1 Look at pages 2 and 3. What is Luke?

- ○ a bike
- ○ a man with a cap
- ○ a yellow truck

2 What does Luke carry?

- ○ many cars
- ○ lots of bikes
- ○ lots of people

3 Look at page 10. What is Luke's problem?

- ○ Luke can not go up the hill.
- ○ Luke is mad.
- ○ Luke has a flat tire.

☞ **4** What does this story teach us?

- ○ Do not go on big hills.
- ○ If we all help, we can fix the problem.
- ○ Bikes are fun to ride.

☞ **5** How do the people help Luke? Use words from the story in your answer.

_____
_____
_____
_____
_____

© Scott Foresman 1

☞ Theme

Read the play *The Three Hares: A Folk Tale from Turkey*. Then answer Numbers 1 through 5.

❶ What does Papa tell the three hares to do?

- ○ dig deep dens
- ○ stay in his den
- ○ watch out for Fox

❷ The first two hares do NOT listen to Papa. Why?

- ○ They like to run from Fox.
- ○ They only listen to Mama.
- ○ They think digging is too much work.

❸ When Fox comes, the two lazy hares

- ○ run to their sister's den.
- ○ go home to Papa.
- ○ are grabbed by Fox.

☞ **❹** What does this play teach us?

- ○ Rest before you work.
- ○ Listen to your dad and mom.
- ○ Stay away from Fox.

☞ **❺** Why are the three hares safe in the blue bunny's den? Use words from the play in your answer.

_____
_____
_____
_____
_____
_____
_____
_____

© Scott Foresman 1

☞ Drawing Conclusions

Read the story *Which Is Which?* Then answer Numbers 1 through 5.

❶ What is Mother Pig's problem?

- ○ All of her babies want to eat.
- ○ All of her babies play in the mud.
- ○ All of her babies look the same.

☞ **❷** Look at pages 6 and 7. Why does Mother Pig say **"Oops"**?

- ○ She can not tell which baby is which.
- ○ She trips and falls all the time.
- ○ She does not know how to say **"oink-oink."**

☞ **❸** Look at page 10. How does Fay feel?

- ○ happy
- ○ upset
- ○ afraid

❹ What does Mother Pig do?

- ○ She dresses the babies in different ways.
- ○ She makes all the pigs stay next to her.
- ○ She curls their tails in different ways.

☞ **❺** Look at pages 14 and 15. What can Mother Pig do now? Use words from the story in your answer.

_____

- - - - - - - - - - - - - - - - - - -

_____

- - - - - - - - - - - - - - - - - - -

_____

- - - - - - - - - - - - - - - - - - -

© Scott Foresman 1

Drawing Conclusions

Read the book *How Crayons Are Made*. Then answer Numbers 1 through 5.

1 How are all crayons ALIKE?

- ○ They are the same size.
- ○ They are the same color.
- ○ They are made the same way.

2 Crayons are made of

- ○ berries.
- ○ wax.
- ○ soap.

3 What happens AFTER the wax gets cold?

- ○ The crayons get hard.
- ○ The wax goes into molds.
- ○ The wax gets soft.

4 Look at pages 8 and 9. You can tell that

- ○ people do not like making crayons.
- ○ many crayons are made.
- ○ only red crayons are made.

5 Look at page 12. What is inside the big boxes?

_____

_____

_____

_____

_____

© Scott Foresman 1

☞ Plot

Read the story *Yes, But.* Then answer Numbers 1 through 5.

☞ **1** What happens FIRST in the story?

- ○ Mouse comes to see Squirrel at her home.
- ○ Squirrel wants to show her new home to her friends.
- ○ Spider makes a big web in Squirrel's home.

2 Squirrel's friends are

- ○ Dog, Cat, and Crow.
- ○ Crow, Mouse, and Spider.
- ○ Mouse, Squirrel, and Frog.

☞ **3** What happens when each friend comes to see Squirrel?

- ○ Each friend changes Squirrel's home.
- ○ Each friend brings food for dinner.
- ○ Each friend helps Squirrel paint her house.

4 Look at page 12. Why is squirrel unhappy?

- ○ Her friends have left her house.
- ○ Her house is falling out of the tree.
- ○ Her things are not where she wants them to be.

☞ **5** How does the story end? Use words from the story in your answer.

_ _

_ _

_ _

© Scott Foresman 1

☞ Plot

Read the story *Mr. Small*. Then answer Numbers 1 through 5.

① What does Mr. Small want to do?

- ○ make a birdhouse
- ○ watch birds
- ○ fly like a bird

② What does Mr. Small make?

- ○ wings, feathers, a beak, a nest
- ○ a kite, a ball, a plane, a ladder
- ○ wings, legs, eyes, feet

③ What do you know about Mr. Small?

- ○ He can fly like a bird.
- ○ He tries very hard.
- ○ He does not like birds.

④ Look at page 15. Why do the birds like Mr. Small?

- ○ He gives them bird food.
- ○ He is very funny.
- ○ He looks like a bird.

⑤ How does the story end? Use words from the story in the answer.

_____

_____

_____

_____

_____

© Scott Foresman 1

ℰ Theme

Read the story *Almost*. Then answer Numbers 1 through 5.

1 Look at page 3. How does Ned feel?

○ afraid
○ glad
○ happy

2 Look at page 12. How does Ted help Ned?

○ Ted gives Ned some water.
○ Ted gives Ned some of his apple.
○ Ted takes some apple from Ned.

3 Look at pages 15 and 16. How does Ned help Ted?

○ He shows him how to jump.
○ He tells him not to be afraid.
○ He helps him get on the seesaw.

ℰ 4 This story tells how Ted and Ned

○ eat apples.
○ help each other.
○ go to the beach.

ℰ 5 What does this story teach us? Use words from the story in your answer.

_____

_____

_____

_____

© Scott Foresman 1

☞ Theme

Read the story *Panda Picture*. Then answer Numbers 1 through 5.

1 The girl thinks she sees a panda

- ○ in a tree.
- ○ at her house.
- ○ all around town.

☞ 2 The girl does NOT think the panda is real. Why?

- ○ It is not right to see a panda in those places.
- ○ There are no pandas in the world.
- ○ A real panda cannot walk.

3 The girl wants to find out if the panda is real so she

- ○ goes on a boat ride.
- ○ keeps looking for it.
- ○ curls her hair.

4 The girl did see a real panda. How do you know?

- ○ A real panda likes to ride a bus.
- ○ A man in the park tells her.
- ○ She took a picture of it.

☞ 5 What does this story teach us? Use words from the story in your answer.

_____

- -

_____

- -

_____

- -

_____

- -

_____

- -

_____

© Scott Foresman 1

Name _____

Drawing Conclusions

Read the story _The Move_. Then answer Numbers 1 through 5.

1 Look at page 2. How does the boy feel about moving?

○ glad
○ happy
○ unhappy

2 The boy will miss

○ his sister Jen.
○ his friend Bill.
○ his dog Sam.

3 Why do the boy's mom and dad want to move?

○ They want a smaller house.
○ They want a bigger house.
○ They want to make new friends.

4 What happens at the new house?

○ The boy makes a new friend.
○ The boy does not like his school.
○ The boy and his dad play ball.

5 Why is the boy happy at the end of the story? Use words from the story in your answer.

_____

_____

_____

_____

_____

© Scott Foresman 1

Name _____

☞ Drawing Conclusions

Read the book *Our Place*. Then answer Numbers 1 through 5.

1 Where is a place for a spider? ☞ **3** Look at pages 6 and 7. The boy says, **"Don't smell that flower."** Why?

   ○ a flower
   ○ a nest
   ○ a web

○ The flower is in the garden.
○ A bee is in the flower.
○ It does not smell good.

2 What eats worms for dinner?

   ○ a rabbit
   ○ a mouse
   ○ a baby bird

☞ **4** Where is a place for us all?

○ Earth
○ the moon
○ the sky

☞ **5** What does this story teach us? Use words from the story in your answer.

_____

_____

_____

_____

_____

© Scott Foresman 1

Answer Key
Leveled Reader Practice

Page 141
1. looks for the animals.
2. hens.
3. ran away.
4. sad.
5. Drawings should show that the animals have been planning a birthday party for the dog.

Page 142
1. Tex has an itch.
2. Horse
3. Horse and Bob do not help Tex.
4. jab them.
5. Drawings should show Bird scratching Tex.

Page 143
1. play
2. Frog gets on top of Cat.
3. Butterfly comes down.
4. five
5. Drawings should show the boy and the five story animals falling down.

Page 144
1. The girl makes a plane.
2. a boat
3. The boy can not see.
4. big.
5. Drawing should show a paper plane, a paper boat, and a paper hat.

Page 145
1. They go up.
2. the bug with the ball.
3. glad
4. Bugs will come down.
5. Drawings should pair: grasshopper/umbrella, caterpillar/ball, ladybug/balloon.

Page 146
1. hide
2. The bird might eat them.
3. It is a bug.
4. The leaf has legs.
5. Drawings might show the bug hopping away or the bird trying to get the bug.

Page 147
1. spring
2. Five comes after four
3. six
4. The frogs see a cat.
5. Drawings should show frogs in a water scene at the edge of a pond or river.

Page 148
1. yellow fish.
2. They can hide.
3. They like to see fish.
4. plants.
5. Drawings should show fish in a large fish tank/aquarium.

Page 149
1. little frogs.
2. to get a pail of water.
3. makes you laugh.
4. funny.
5. Drawings should show Jack and Jill swimming in a pail of water.

Page 150
1. at night.
2. in a can
3. a pen.
4. tells you about real animals.
5. Drawings should show the raccoon running away from a skunk in a cave.

Page 151
1. eat.
2. Stop! Eat!
3. They eat the leaves.
4. They see the light.
5. Drawings might show the armadillos running away.

Page 152
1. bed time
2. on a farm.
3. owls and frogs
4. He wants to hear them sing.
5. Drawings should show the boy smiling.

Page 153
1. Kit
2. They like to play.
3. Kit is not on Tim's team.
4. Kit kicks the ball in the net.
5. Drawings should show Tim playing soccer or helping Kit or another child.

Page 154
1. the yellow cab, the boy, and the mom
2. turn
3. They can go slow.
4. the boy and his mom
5. Drawings should show a hand with a palm out to indicate *STOP* and two hands in a sweeping motion to show *GO*.

Page 155
1. find holes
2. Hic! Hic! Hic!
3. scared
4. Pat
5. Drawings should show Pat holding a popped balloon.

Page 156
1. her old things
2. it is too small
3. happy
4. to share things
5. Drawings might show the sisters playing together with the things pictured.

© Scott Foresman 1

Page 157
1. jumping rope
2. They are good at jumping rope.
3. She misses.
4. She jumped and jumped.
5. Drawings should show the girl's dog.

Page 158
1. a sleeping pig
2. work.
3. Pig will not help.
4. food
5. Drawings should show Pig eating.

Page 159
1. talk.
2. Polly can say *cracker*.
3. The dog is talking.
4. Molly, Polly, Dad
5. Drawings should show a parrot, a dog, and a cat.

Page 160
1. at the zoo.
2. what animals like to eat.
3. the bear, the elephant, and the giraffe.
4. She likes to work with animals.
5. Drawings should show one of the following: elephant/apples, bear/fish, giraffe/leaves, fox/carrots, monkey/bananas, zebra/hay, fawn/milk.

Page 161
1. soap
2. He wants to wash his bike.
3. a bike
4. Mama and Papa
5. Drawings should show messy, dirty family members.

Page 162
1. the queen
2. letters
3. in the pool
4. They get in the pool.
5. Drawings should show the queen having fun in the pool or in some other way.

Page 163
1. teach the pig how to dance
2. They get up and dance again.
3. happy.
4. The pig likes to dance.
5. Drawings should show the girl and the pig happy or tired from dancing.

Page 164
1. eat peas.
2. please!
3. play with her toys
4. funny.
5. Drawings might show the baby with her bib or hands covering her stubborn-looking face.

Page 165
1. jumping rope
2. Baby and the dog
3. They all fall down.
4. could happen in real life.
5. Drawings should show all family members jumping rope again.

Page 166
1. his dog
2. He wants to make his bike look good.
3. Biff runs with the red ribbon.
4. could happen in real life.
5. Drawings should show a dog doing something that could not happen in real life.

Page 167
1. on Mother's Day
2. Kitty makes breakfast for Mom.
3. Kitty
4. Real cats do not make food.
5. Drawings might show Mom and Kitty cleaning up the mess.

Page 168
1. play ball
2. jump
3. She tells him to jump again and again.
4. He turns into a bat.
5. Drawings should show Bat flying and/or catching a ball.

Page 169
1. It is Father's Day
2. Ben thinks Dad will like it.
3. the hug
4. Ben is nice to his dad.
5. Drawings should show a card, clay cat, or breakfast food.

Page 170
1. Linn goes to karate class.
2. She loves karate class.
3. She kicks and chops.
4. Thank you for the class.
5. Drawings might show Linn bowing, kicking, chopping, blocking, or yelling.

Page 171
1. to the fair
2. They happen from 2–4 p.m.
3. It helps you tell time.
4. It is the end of the day and the book.
5. Drawings should show a clock with hands indicating 4 o'clock.

Page 172
1. about Zulu dancers.
2. the brother
3. fast and hard
4. He thinks about being a dancer.
5. Drawings should show the boy wearing the costume of a Zulu dancer.

Page 173
1. three bowls, three chairs, and three beds.
2. They count four bowls, four chairs, and four beds.
3. four bears
4. This is not where they live.
5. Drawings should show three brown bears doing something in their own house.

Page 174
1. It could not happen in real life.
2. to scare the animals away
3. He is all alone.
4. They help Long Tom to fly.
5. Drawings should show cows, raccoons, and crows.

© Scott Foresman 1

Page 175
1. tell knock-knock jokes
2. fruit.
3. Real chimps can eat fruit.
4. a fruit salad
5. Drawings should show chimps painting, cooking, talking, or living in their own house.

Page 176
1. He needs to dress warmly.
2. A bunny talks in this story.
3. He is wearing too many things.
4. eat a leaf
5. Drawings should show bunny's mother helping him up and/or taking off a layer of Bunny's clothing.

Page 177
1. to the playground.
2. She is going to a ranch.
3. She will think of the bed first.
4. a book and flowers
5. She is going to the beach.

Page 178
1. by plane
2. Grandpa played with the shells on the other days.
3. He fills the shells with bits of paper.
4. The bits of paper fall on Grandpa.
5. "Only for fun."

Page 179
1. a T-shirt.
2. The girl wore the T-shirt.
3. seven
4. She puts it on her panda.
5. She is bigger.

Page 180
1. windows, doors, lamps, beds.
2. everyone
3. three hours
4. She likes to live in both houses.
5. Both are full of friends.

Page 181
1. Mary gets dressed up.
2. Mary goes for a walk.
3. to see how she looks
4. Mary falls in the water.
5. Possible answer: Mary gets wet. Mary goes home.

Page 182
1. a fox in the desert.
2. food and water
3. She wakes up.
4. She looks and waits.
5. Possible answers: The fox gets the lizard. The fox eats the lizard.

Page 183
1. They are going on a walk.
2. They slap the bugs.
3. They see a skunk.
4. a snake on the walk.
5. She helps him climb a rock.

Page 184
1. It has been too hot and dry.
2. Rain comes from big black clouds.
3. It starts to rain.
4. A boy could not catch a cloud with a rope.
5. Possible answers: They are dancing because they have rain. They are dancing because they are happy.

Page 185
1. real pandas.
2. in China
3. things an animal does again and again
4. things pandas like to do
5. Students may write about one of the following habits: Pandas like to climb, hide, swim, slide, sit, play, eat, roll, creep, or sleep.

Page 186
1. Lilly Pup can not find a quiet place to read at home.
2. to a quiet spot
3. She goes to sleep.
4. She hears her family looking for her.
5. Lilly Pup likes to read.

Page 187
1. why possums have bare tails.
2. we should listen to our mothers.
3. The fire burns his tail.
4. Little Possum got too close to the fire.
5. Little Possum gets a bee sting.

Page 188
1. a girl who lives far away
2. She likes the many little beads.
3. She sends it to Robin.
4. her mother's sister
5. Robin smiles. Robin thinks of the girl far away.

Page 189
1. how to paint your face.
2. Paint your face like a clown.
3. get a brush, water, and paint.
4. It helps you see how to paint the face.
5. Put paint on the face.

Page 190
1. a toymaker
2. a workshop.
3. draws a picture of the new toy.
4. an airplane
5. He cleans up his workshop.

Page 191
1. a yellow truck
2. lots of bikes
3. Luke can not go up the hill.
4. If we all help, we can fix the problem.
5. Possible answer: The people ride the bikes up the hill. Then Luke can go to the top.

Page 192
1. dig deep dens
2. They think digging is too much work.
3. run to their sister's den.
4. Listen to your dad and mom.
5. They are safe because she dug her den deep and safe.

Page 193
1. All of her babies look the same.
2. She can not tell which baby is which.
3. upset
4. She curls their tails in different ways.
5. She can tell which pig is which.

© Scott Foresman 1

Page 194
1. They are made the same way.
2. wax.
3. The crayons get hard.
4. many crayons are made.
5. There are boxes of crayons inside the big boxes.

Page 195
1. Squirrel wants to show her new home to her friends.
2. Crow, Mouse, and Spider.
3. Each friend changes Squirrel's home.
4. Her things are not where she wants them to be.
5. Squirrel asks her friends to put her things back to where she wants them.

Page 196
1. fly like a bird
2. wings, feathers, a beak, a nest
3. He tries very hard.
4. He looks like a bird.
5. Mr. Small does not fly. He is happy because he has many bird friends.

Page 197
1. afraid
2. Ted gives Ned some of his apple.
3. He helps him get on the seesaw.
4. help each other.
5. Answers will vary, but children should use words and details from the story to identify a basic theme such as "Friends help one another," or "You should help your friends."

Page 198
1. all around town.
2. It is not right to see a panda in those places.
3. keeps looking for it.
4. She took a picture of it.
5. Possible answers: Sometimes we do not believe what we see. Sometimes things that "couldn't be" will happen for a good reason.

Page 199
1. unhappy
2. his friend Bill.
3. They want a bigger house.
4. The boy makes a new friend.
5. Possible answers: He likes his new house and school. He has a new friend. His old friend can come over to play.

Page 200
1. a web
2. a baby bird
3. A bee is in the flower.
4. Earth
5. Possible answers: There is a place for everything on Earth. Each animal has its own place on Earth.

© Scott Foresman 1

Scott Foresman Leveling System

Stage	Language Structure	Illustrations (Art and Photos)	Vocabulary, Concepts, Content, and Genre	Text Format and Features (Book Length, Size, and Layout)	Phonics and Word Study
Beginning Independent Readers (K, 1.1)	repetitive patterns with one word substitutions, rhyme, and repetition	simple illustrations, consistent picture-to-text sequence	familiar objects and/or common experiences, many words are pictured	single line of text per page; large, clear type size and typeface; small number of words per selection	one syllable words or high frequency words predominate
Early/Novice Leveled Readers Grade 1: 1A–30A	memorable repetitive language patterns throughout, predictable forms	strong support for text, consistent picture-to-text sequence	easily understood concepts, short words	short selections with few characters; single line of text per page; large, clear type size and typeface; small number of words per selection	focus on consonants, rhyming patterns, phonograms, and phonetically regular words; greater use of high frequency words
Novice/Developing Leveled Readers Grade 1: 1B–30B Grade 2: 31A–60A	some repeated language, consistent sentence structure	pictures reinforce overall meaning	short words, words with similar visual patterns	short selections with few characters, one to two lines of text per page, clear and consistent type size and typeface	
Developing/Fluent Leveled Readers Grade 1: Level C Grade 2: 31B–60B Grade 3: 61A–90A	mix of speech and language patterns, some sentence variety	some text support to reinforce meaning, moderate picture-to-text match	story-like but short episodes, stories become more complex with several characters	more lines of text per page, consistent arrangement of text on page	focus on short vowels, long vowels, consonant blends, and digraphs

Scott Foresman Leveling System

Stage	Language Structure	Illustrations (Art and Photos)	Vocabulary, Concepts, Content, and Genre	Text Format and Features (Book Length, Size, and Layout)	Phonics and Word Study
Fluent Leveled Readers Grade 2: Level C Grade 3: 61B–90B Grade 4: 91A–120A	greater variety in sentence structure, some examples of compound sentences	illustrations reinforce overall meaning, convey setting and atmosphere	more story-like with longer events, several characters, some specialized vocabulary, increase in content-area words, photos add support for nonfiction selections	longer selections with varied genres and literary styles, increase in nonfiction selections	focus on inflected endings, compound words, plurals, r-controlled vowels, and long and short vowels
Fluent/Proficient Leveled Readers Grade 3: Level C Grade 4: 91B–120B Grade 5: 121A–150A	written language forms and literary language predominate, greater variety in sentence structure, many more compound sentences	few illustrations to reinforce overall meaning, and convey setting and atmosphere	more specialized topics and vocabulary, increase in number of vocabulary words, photos add support for nonfiction selections	longer selections with varied genres and literary styles, increase in nonfiction selections	emphasis is on multisyllabic words
Proficient Leveled Readers Grade 4: Level C Grade 5: 121B–150B Grade 6: 151A–180A	well-developed events, more examples of literary language, greater variety in sentence structure, many compound sentences	varied styles to support overall meaning; convey setting, atmosphere, and/or mood; partial pages with illustrations	more specialized topics and vocabulary, increase in number of vocabulary words	smaller type size fits full page, longer selections with varied genres and literary styles, increase in nonfiction selections	many examples of multisyllabic words
Proficient Leveled Readers Grade 5: Level C Grade 6: 151B–180B Grade 6: Level C	well-developed events, more examples of literary language, greater variety in sentence structure, many compound sentences, more sophisticated language structures	partial pages with illustrations, minimum picture support	increase in number of vocabulary words, challenging vocabulary incorporated	smaller type size fills full page; complex stories that describe setting, characters, problem(s), and resolution(s) in more detail	many examples of multisyllabic words

Observation Checklist/Progress Report

Student's Name _____ **Date** _____

Behaviors Observed	Always (Fluent)	Usually (Developing)	Sometimes (Novice)	Rarely (Beginning)

Print Knowledge/Beginning Reading Skills

	Always (Fluent)	Usually (Developing)	Sometimes (Novice)	Rarely (Beginning)
Holds book correctly				
Identifies parts of a book and their functions				
Understands concept of letter, word, sentence, and paragraph				
Tracks print correctly				
Matches spoken to printed words				

Reading Strategies and Skills

	Always (Fluent)	Usually (Developing)	Sometimes (Novice)	Rarely (Beginning)
Uses prior knowledge and preview to understand what book is about				
Makes predictions and checks them while reading				
Uses picture clues to decode words and construct meaning				
Uses letter-sound knowledge to decode words				
Uses context clues to figure out meanings of new words				
Self-corrects while reading				
Reads at an approapriate reading rate				
Reads with appropriate intonation and stress				
Uses fix-up strategies				
Identifies story elements: character, setting, plot structure, theme				
Summarizes plot or main ideas accurately				
Uses target comprehension skill to understand the text better				
Responds thoughtfully about the text				

Reading Behaviors and Attitudes

	Always (Fluent)	Usually (Developing)	Sometimes (Novice)	Rarely (Beginning)
Enjoys listening to stories				
Chooses reading as a free-time activity				
Reads with sustained interest and attention				
Participates in discussion about books				

© Scott Foresman 1

Taking a Running Record

A running record is an assessment of a child's oral reading accuracy and oral reading fluency. Reading accuracy is based on the number of words read correctly. Reading fluency is based on the reading rate (the number of words read per minute) and the degree to which the child reads with a "natural flow."

How to Measure Reading Accuracy

1. Choose a grade-level text of about 80 to 120 words that is unfamiliar to the child.

2. Make a copy of the text for yourself. Make a copy for the child or have the child read aloud from a book.

3. Give the child the text and have the child read aloud. (You may wish to tape-record the child's reading for later evaluation.)

4. On your copy of the text, mark any miscues or errors the child makes while reading. See the running record sample on page 9, which shows how to identify and mark miscues.

5. Count the total number of words in the text and the total number of errors made by the child. Note: If a child makes the same error more than once, such as mispronouncing the same word multiple times, count it as one error. Self-corrections do not count as actual errors. Use the following formula to calculate the percentage score, or accuracy rate:

$$\frac{\text{Total Number of Words} - \text{Total Number of Errors}}{\text{Total Number of Words}} \times 100 = \text{percentage score}$$

Interpreting the Results

- A child who reads **98–100%** of the words correctly is reading at an **independent level** and may need more challenging texts.

- A child who reads **91–97%** of the words correctly is reading at an **instructional level** and will likely benefit from guided instruction.

- A child who reads **90% or less** of the words correctly is reading at a **frustrational level** and may benefit most from targeted instruction with lower-level texts and intervention.

See the Scott Foresman Leveling System on pages 205 and 206 to help you select materials that are appropriate for the child's reading level.

How to Measure Reading Rate

1. Follow Steps 1–3 above.

2. Note the exact times when the child begins and finishes reading.

3. Use the following formula to calculate the number of words per minute (wpm), or reading rate:

$$\frac{\text{Total Number of Words Read}}{\text{Total Number of Seconds}} \times 60 = \text{words per minute}$$

Interpreting the Results

An appropriate rate is roughly equal to the child age × 10, plus or minus 10. For example, a 7-year-old child should read 60–80 words per minute.

Scott Foresman

Reading

Independent Reader Resource Guide

Table of Contents

The following activities can be used with Independent Readers for the children on an independent basis or as small-group activities.

Creating Big Books

Children can work in small groups to create a big book from any of the Independent Readers. After the big book has been put together, encourage a volunteer to read it to the rest of the class.

Creating a Character Mural

Introduce this activity at the beginning of the year. Invite children to create an Independent Reader character mural. Use a large piece of butcher paper and place it on an accessible wall. Title it "Character Mural." As children read each of the Independent Readers, have them pick out a character from the story and re-create it on the butcher paper. Children can re-create the characters using paints, crayons, magazine pictures, noodles, beads, buttons, and so on.

Creating an Audio/Video Library

Audiocassette Ideas Record school helpers (principals, custodians, parent volunteers, upper grade "Big Buddies," and so on) reading each of the Independent Readers on audiocassette. The audiocassettes can then be left at the Listening Center for children to use. If possible, place a photo of each reader, the audiocassette, and the Independent Reader in a bag for storage.

Record children reading the Independent Readers. Label each audiocassette with the child's name and the date. You can use this at a later date to assess children's growth in their ability to read text, their ability to decode words, and their fluency.

Videotape Ideas Record children reading the Independent Readers on videotape. Label the videotape with the date and the children's names.

You can use these recordings to assess children's changes in their reading ability, their ability to decode words, their fluency, their ability to track text from left to right.

Creating Charts

Work with children to create various types of charts and graphs that incorporate the Independent Readers. For example:

- Create a tally chart that tells how many stories have an animal on the cover or how many have people on the cover.
- Create a sorting chart that classifies the covers by person, place, or thing.
- Create a picture graph. Given the choice of three Independent Readers, ask children which is their favorite reader. Ask them to draw a picture of a character from their favorite reader. Place each picture under the appropriate column. Children can count the number of pictures in each column to determine the class favorite.
- Create a bar graph. Given the choice of the first twelve Independent Readers, make a graph to show which readers have stories that could really happen and which are make-believe stories.

Writing

Invite children to draw a picture of their favorite part of the story and then dictate or write a sentence about it in their journals or on the computer.

Have children use the pattern in the text to write their own version of the story by changing only a word or two.

Children can rewrite endings or even continue the stories.

Using High-Frequency Words Give children two high-frequency words from the story and then ask them to write a sentence using those words. As children become accustomed to writing a sentence with the two high-frequency words, add another two words and ask them to write two sentences. Keep increasing the number of high-frequency words and the number of sentences.

can

is

like

and

Drama

You may wish to provide children with props to help them dramatize any of the Independent Readers. Children can create new story lines by acting out the story using a different setting or adding new characters.

What happens to the rest of the group while you are working with the guided reading group? While working with a group during guided reading, the rest of the children should be involved with reading activities that are meaningful and that support your objectives for the skills you are teaching. The work stations described below can be developed for those children who are not working on guided reading.

Additional information for setting up and maintaining work stations can be found in the Scott Foresman Reading Teacher's Editions.

How long should each activity last? As you are explaining each activity you can help children understand how long they should stay there. Recommended time varies from the beginning of the year (less time) to the end of the year (more time). The average time recommended is 15 minutes.

How often should the stations be changed? You may wish to vary the stations to keep the children's interest. For example: once a week, change the story at the listening center or add more books to the Independent Reading Work Station.

Listening Work Station Children can listen to stories as they track the print on he book. Refer to Extend the Reading on page 148 for more information on Listening Work Station Ideas.

Technology Work Station There are software programs that allow children to create their own books. If this software is not available to you, allow children to create the text on the computer. Then when children move to the art center they can draw the illustrations to match their text.

Writing and Language Work Station Materials: children's writing journals, various kinds of paper, pencils, crayons

Children can retell stories or write their own versions of the Independent Reader stories. The high-frequency word cards for that week can be displayed for children to use so that they can include the words in their stories.

Independent Reading Work Station Provide children with various choices to "read" on their own; (for example) Independent Readers, favorite big books, and read alouds.

Cross-Curricular Work Station You can provide various cross-curricular work stations such as art, science, or math. These cross-curricular work stations can provide children with specific tasks or provide open-ended exploration.

Assessment

Record the date each child is able to independently read the books on the following Assessment Chart. Make a copy of the chart for each unit. Record the Independent Reader numbers and names on the top rows and the children's names in the first column.

Student Name	Independent Reader #	Independent Reader #	Independent Reader #	Independent Reader #	Independent Reader #	Independent Reader #
1						
2						
3						
4						
5						
6						
7						
8						
9						
10						
11						
12						
13						
14						
15						
16						
17						
18						
19						
20						
21						
22						
23						
24						

Grade 1/Unit 1

Using the Grade 1/Unit 1 Independent Reader Resource Guide

Skills to Reinforce and Review

High-Frequency Words Use the Independent Readers to review all of the Kindergarten tested high-frequency words.

Comprehension Skill The comprehension skills covered in Grade 1 Unit 1 can be reinforced using the Independent Readers. The Guiding Comprehension feature includes teaching suggestions for the comprehension skill taught that particular week.

Other Skills Each Independent Reader can be used to teach other skills. These skills include: analyzing word structure; noting sentence punctuation and other conventions of print; recognizing categories of words such as number words, color words, nouns, verbs, and adjectives.

The following is an explanation of the teaching suggestions you will find for each of the Grade 1/Unit 1 Independent Readers.

Picture Walk Preview the stories by reading the title, the author's name, and the illustrator's name with children. Invite children to scan the illustrations to predict what the story will be about.

Building Vocabulary This activity provides children with opportunities to recall high-frequency words by using word cards in various ways: matching the word cards to the corresponding words on the pages, finding the same words on the ABC wall, or reading the word cards. These activities help children to develop a routine to review vocabulary and to improve their reading.

Guiding Comprehension Teaching suggestions are given for checking reading comprehension.

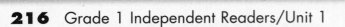

1.1

Written by Judy Nelson

Skill Reinforcement and Review

- **High-Frequency Words:** *I, see, a, red, blue, yellow*
- **Comprehension Skill:** Predicting
- **Other Skills:** words for colors; naming words (nouns)

Picture Walk Display the cover of *Rain* and help children read the title. Remind them that the cover also gives other information about the book. Ask someone to name the author and illustrator of the story and to tell about the picture. Then encourage children to look at the pictures and predict what they think the book is about. Remind them to use the picture clues to preview and predict.

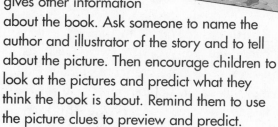

Building Vocabulary Show the word cards: *I, see, a, red, blue,* and *yellow.* Tell children that these are some of the words they will see in *Rain.* Invite volunteers to match the word cards to the corresponding words on the pages.

Guiding Comprehension After children read pages 2 and 3, have them predict what the child in the picture will do next. Then let them read the rest of the story independently. Check comprehension by having them retell the story.

1.2

Look and See!

Written by Christine Rakow

Skill Reinforcement and Review

- **High-Frequency Words:** *can, at, look, the, my, and*
- **Comprehension Skill:** Classifying
- **Other Skills:** naming words (nouns); action words (verbs)

Picture Walk Display the Independent Reader *Look and See!* Read the title with children. Point to and read the names of the author and illustrator. Ask children to point to the name of the person who wrote the book and the name of the person who drew the pictures. Then point to the title again and ask a volunteer to tell what he or she thinks the title means. Have children look at the pictures and predict what they think the story is about.

Building Vocabulary Show the word cards: *can, at, look, the, my,* and *and.* Tell children that these are some of the words they will see in *Look and See!* Invite volunteers to find the same words on the ABC Wall.

Guiding Comprehension Ask children to read page 2 and begin a list of words that name the things in the story. Begin the list with *child* and *dog.* Remind children that the child looks and sees the dog just as the title says. Have children read the rest of the story to see who "looks and sees" other things.

1.3

My Big Family

Written by Sally Terkel

Skill Reinforcement and Review

- **High-Frequency Words:** *big, it, is, in, little, have*
- **Comprehension Skill:** Main Idea
- **Other Skills:** adjectives; naming words (nouns)

Picture Walk Show the cover of the book and help children read the title *My Big Family.* Read the names on the cover and ask which name is the author and which is the illustrator. Then encourage children to tell what the book is  about based on the title of the book and the pictures. Have them tell about the picture on the cover and identify the people and the action in the selection.

Building Vocabulary Show the word cards: *big, it, is, in, little,* and *have.* Tell children that these are some of the words they will see in *My Big Family.* Invite volunteers to match the word cards to the corresponding words on the pages.

Guiding Comprehension After children read page 2, have them name the things they know about the family based on the girl in the picture. Then let children read the rest of the story independently. Check their comprehension by having children retell the story.

1.4

Do You See?

Written by Stefanie Langer

Skill Reinforcement and Review

- **High-Frequency Words:** *not, you, do, like, to, that*
- **Comprehension Skill:** Fact/Fantasy
- **Other Skills:** adjectives; nouns (naming words); verbs (action words)

Picture Walk Display the Independent Reader *Do You See?* and read the title with children. Then point to and read the names of the author and illustrator. Review the terms  *author* and *illustrator* with children and confirm that they understand each term. Ask them to look at the pictures and tell about what they see.

Building Vocabulary Show the word cards: *not, you, do, like, to,* and *that.* Tell children that these are some of the words they will see in *Do You See?* Invite volunteers to find the same words on the ABC Wall.

Guiding Comprehension Read page 2 together and have children discuss the purpose of the bubble shapes by the child's head. If necessary, explain that the child's thoughts are printed in the bubble shapes. Then let children read the story independently.

1.5 What Can We Get?

Written by Alex Adams

Skill Reinforcement and Review

- **High-Frequency Words:** *get, what, we, one, two, three*
- **Comprehension Skill:** Sequence
- **Other Skills:** words for numbers; naming words (nouns)

Picture Walk Display the book and help children read the title *What Can We Get?* Ask someone to point to the names of the author and illustrator of the story. Show several pages and invite children to tell about the pictures and use the information in the picture and the title to predict what they think the story will be about.

Building Vocabulary Show the word cards: *get, what, we, one, two,* and *three*. Tell children that these are some of the words they will see in *What Can We Get?* Invite volunteers to read the word cards.

Guiding Comprehension Read pages 2 and 3 together and ask children how the title fits the story. Encourage them to predict what the children will do next. Then let children read the rest of the story independently. Check their comprehension by having children retell the story.

1.6 Where Is Bear?

Written by Chris Kiel

Skill Reinforcement and Review

- **High-Frequency Words:** *up, but, go, where, here, am*
- **Comprehension Skill:** Recall and Retell
- **Other Skills:** adjectives; naming words (nouns); action words (verbs)

Picture Walk Display the Independent Reader *Where Is Bear?* and read the title with children. Then point to and read the names of the author and illustrator. Review the terms *author* and *illustrator* with children. Ask children to look at the animal on the cover and tell about what they see. Show several pages and ask children to look at the pictures and predict what they think the book is about.

Building Vocabulary Show the word cards: *up, but, go, where, here,* and *am*. Tell children that these are some of the words they will see in *Where Is Bear?* Invite volunteers to find the same words on the ABC Wall.

Guiding Comprehension Read page 2 together and have children explain why the animals are running away from the tree. Remind them that Bear is covering his eyes and invite them to think about a game that might fit the clues they see (hide-and-seek). Then let children read the story independently.